THE NEW INTERNATIONAL COMMENTARY ON THE
NEW TESTAMENT   —F. F. Bruce, *General Editor*

THE EPISTLE OF PAUL TO THE PHILIPPIANS

THE EPISTLE OF PAUL TO THE PHILIPPIANS

THE ENGLISH TEXT WITH INTRODUCTION, EXPOSITION AND NOTES

by

JAC. J. MÜLLER
Professor of New Testament
The Theological Seminary, Stellenbosch, South Africa

THE EPISTLE OF PAUL TO THE PHILIPPIANS
BY JAC. J. MÜLLER, TH. D., D.D.

WM. B. EERDMANS PUBLISHING COMPANY
GRAND RAPIDS, MICHIGAN, U.S.A.

First published June 1955 as part of
THE EPISTLES OF PAUL
TO THE PHILIPPIANS AND TO PHILEMON

Reprinted, May 1988

ISBN 0-8028-2188-X

PHOTOLITHOPRINTED BY EERDMANS PRINTING COMPANY
GRAND RAPIDS, MICHIGAN, UNITED STATES OF AMERICA

FOREWORD

In introducing Jacobus J. Müller to the readers of this Commentary, I may be indulged if I begin by recalling my delightful contacts with him, E. P. Groenewald and other South Africans at the Free University of Amsterdam when we were fellow-students some twenty-five years ago. The contacts with Groenewald were somewhat more intimate in view of our common specialization in the New Testament field, but Müller was hardly less interested in the New Testament though he was taking his graduate work in systematic theology. A contributory factor no doubt was that, in addition to his undergraduate work in the arts and his regular theological course in Stellenbosch, he had also qualified for an M. A. in Greek. Though I have not seen him in the years that followed, I still have vivid recollections of his alert and genial personality.

In 1931 he qualified for the doctorate at Amsterdam with a dissertation on *The Kenotic Theory in Post-Reformation Theology*. Returning to his own country he served as a pastor for about fifteen years, during which time he earned a D.D. degree at the University of South Africa at Pretoria upon the basis of a thesis on *The Essence of Christian Sectarianism*. Extraordinary evidence of the esteem in which he came to be held was provided in 1945 when he was elected to two professorships, one in systematic theology in the theological faculty of the University of Pretoria and the other in New Testament in the large Seminary in Stellenbosch. He chose to accept the latter and has labored there successfully for more than a decade. Among his several literary productions, in addition to those referred to above, special mention may be made of a topical and practical commentary on the first six Epistles of Paul which was published in 1952 under the title *Grace to You.*

In view of Dr. Müller's known interest in and specialized knowledge of the great christological passage in Philippians 2, it seemed advantageous to invite him to undertake the commentary upon this Epistle. I anticipate that those who share this special interest will not be disappointed with this decision. But his treatment of the entire Epistle is not less competent and rewarding. Besides there pervades the scholarly exegetical discussion of specific problems and details a sense of the relevancy of the Pauline message he is expounding to the practical interests and needs of his readers, and this in turn reflects the vitality and warmth of the author's personal Christian profession.

Finally it seems appropriate to comment briefly upon a particularly happy feature of the development of *The New International Commentary on the New Testament* as a whole. This is the consideration that the editor has been permitted to have cordial personal contacts with all or nearly all the contributors over a period of many years. The basic and indispensable ingredient of the cooperation has been our essential agreement as to the Christian faith itself. But the ties of Christian brotherhood and friendship rooted in our common faith, which have been established in the good providence of God, have added immeasurably to the joys and fruitfulness of this fellowship in labor. This feature, though not unique so far as Dr. Müller is concerned, has been conspicuously present in this instance, and it is a pleasure to speak of his invariably responsive and gracious spirit in connection with our correspondence regarding this volume.

N. B. STONEHOUSE,
Editor

Philadelphia,
January, 1955

CONTENTS

ABBREVIATIONS

AV	—	Authorised Version (1611)
ASV	—	American Standard Version (1901)
Bl.-Debr.	—	*Grammatik des neutestamentlichen Griechisch* (Blass-Debrunner)
Cremer	—	*Biblico-Theological Lexicon of New Testament Greek*, 4th edition
CE	—	*Christelijke Encyclopaedie*
ICC	—	*International Critical Commentary*
Kittel	—	*Theologisches Wörterbuch zum Neuen Testament* (TWNT)
LXX	—	Septuagint
RGG	—	*Die Religion in Geschichte und Gegenwart*, 2nd Ed.
RSV	—	Revised Standard Version (1946)
Str.-B.	—	*Kommentar zum Neuen Testament au: Talmud und Midrasch*, by Strack and Billerbeck
TR	—	Textus Receptus

Note: Upon the death of Ned B. Stonehouse, November 18, 1962, F. F. Bruce accepted the publishers' invitation to become General Editor of this series of New Testament commentaries begun under the very able and faithful scholarship of Professor Stonehouse.

The Publishers

The Scripture text used in this commentary is that of the American Standard Version of 1901. This text is printed in full for the sake of readers who do not read Greek; the expositions are, however, based upon the Greek text.

INTRODUCTION

THE EPISTLE OF PAUL TO THE PHILIPPIANS

INTRODUCTION

I

The Church Addressed

The Letter is addressed to "the saints in Christ Jesus who are at Philippi" (1:1), the first city on European soil where a Christian Church was founded by Paul, namely on his second missionary journey (Acts 16). At its foundation Paul was accompanied by Timothy, Silas and Luke. Luke narrates the remarkable conversions of Lydia and the gaoler which took place there, as well as the ill-treatment and imprisonment of Paul and Silas, following a riot of the mob.

On his third journey Paul again visited the Church (Acts 20; comp. 2 Cor. 2 and 7), an undertaking which was easily possible, Philippi being situated on the high road between Asia Minor, Greece and Rome.

A very intimate relation seems to have existed between the apostle and the Church, where the first fruits of Europe were gathered by him for Christendom. The Church consisted for the major part of gentile Christians, was small and poor but helpful and generous. On several earlier occasions they sent pecuniary gifts to Paul (Phil 4:15, 16; 2 Cor. 11:9), as also now again during his imprisonment (Phil. 4:10, 14), while they also contributed towards the poor in Jerusalem (2 Cor. 8).

II

Occasion and Purpose

The occasion for writing the Letter was the receipt of a gift from the Church at Philippi, which was brought over

13

by Epaphroditus to the apostle in captivity (Phil. 4:14, 18; 2:25). For this token of love he wished to express his thanks.[1]

The return of Epaphroditus to the Church—after a serious illness from which he had just recovered (2:26—28)—afforded the apostle the opportunity not only gratefully to acknowledge the receipt of the gift but also to inform the Church of his own circumstances in captivity[2] and of the turn taken in the lawsuit which was nearing its end (1:12—26). He also could send the Church some practical Christian admonitions and exhort them to humility, steadfastness and unanimity (2:3—5; 3:2, 3; 4:1, 2; 1:27—30).

III

Authorship and Integrity

The Letter itself asserts the authorship of Paul (1:1), and there is nothing in the Letter, linguistic or historical, which can cause any doubt as to its authenticity.[3]

---

[1] "The Epistle is the Apostle's receipt in acknowledgment of the token of love" (Feine-Behm, *Einleitung in das N. T.* 8te Aufl., 1936, p. 173).

[2] Zahn, *Introduction to the N. T.* (Eng. Trans., 1909, Vol. I, p. 525) regards the Epistle as Paul's immediate reply to a Letter he had just received from Philippi as a result of an earlier writing of his to them, according to 3:1. Indications that the Epistle to the Philippians is a reply to a letter sent by that Church are looked for in 1:12, 1:19, 1:25f., 2:26, 3:1, 2, 4:10—13. The grounds for this view are, however, insufficient and unconvincing, although more correspondence between Paul and the Church than that which is in our possession could have taken place.

[3] Although Timothy—fellow-founder of the Church and now companion of Paul in his imprisonment—is mentioned as associated in

Early and strong evidence regarding the existence and genuineness of the Letter can be adduced. Clemens Romanus (in his Letter to Corinth) already alludes to it, as well as Ignatius (in his Letter to Smyrna). Polycarp (in his Letter to Philippi) reminds the Philippians of the Letter (or Letters) which Paul had written to them. Irenaeus quotes from it, as being words of Paul. With Clemens Alexandrinus and Tertullian quotations from the Letter abound. It found its place in Marcion's Apostolicon as well as in the Muratorian Canon as one of the Letters of Paul. The Letter is therefore very well accredited.

"One would suppose", (thus Zahn)[4] "that the inimitable freshness of feeling betrayed in every line of this Letter, the naturalness . . . the large number of facts hard to invent . . . the strong external evidence, particularly the evidence of the Philippian letter of Polycarp, a disciple of one of the Apostles—might have safeguarded Philippians more even than the other Epistles of Paul against the suspicion of being the product of a later period."

Notwithstanding, however, the authenticity was disputed by the Tübingen School and a few of the later radical theologians, who took this as a "Unionspaulinismus", i.e. an attempt by a later disciple of Paul to reconcile the Jewish-Christian and the Gentile-Christian parties in the Church.[5]

---

sending the Letter, it is throughout written in the 1st person singular, and Paul alone is addressing them.

[4] *Op cit.*, p. 556. Cf. Kennedy, Comm. on Phil., in *Exp. Gr. Test.*, p. 407: "Perhaps no Pauline epistle bears more conclusively the stamp of authenticity."

[5] So, amongst others, Baur, Volkmar, Holsten. Euodia and Syntyche in Phil. 4:2 were accordingly regarded as symbolical names for the Jewish and Gentile Christian parties, who were to be urged towards unanimity.

Of such a contrast or such parties in the Church, however, there is no mention whatsoever in the Letter. And the whole is undeniably Pauline in language and style, trend of thought and manner of presentation.

Thiessen[6] summarises the objections brought in against its authenticity as follows: (1) "Traces of imitation in the Epistle"—which, however, appears unacceptable by virtue of the warmth and artlessness evident everywhere in the Epistle; (2) "Ecclesiastical anachronisms", viz. that Paul could not yet have made mention of "bishops and deacons" (1:1), as was possible in the later ecclesiastical organisation. But the fact is that Paul had already appointed "elders" on his first journey (Acts 14:21—23), and had already used the appellation of "bishops" earlier for the elders of Ephesus (Acts 20:28). Rom. 12:7 already refers to the service rendered by deacons, and the institution of the deaconship is even older than that of the eldership (Acts 6); (3) "Echoes of gnostic ideas," especially with regard to the kenosis of Christ (2:7). His idea of the kenosis is supposed to have been derived from Valentinian.[7] Apart from the fact, however, that Paul on four other occasions and in different connections makes mention of a kenosis (Rom. 4:14, 1 Cor. 1:17, 1 Cor. 9:15, 2 Cor. 9:3), Paul's Christology, as taught in Phil. 2:5—8,—although more comprehensive than elsewhere—is nevertheless the same as we have in 2 Cor. 8:9 and Col. 1:13—19. (4) "Doctrinal differences from the recognised Epistles of Paul" (Gal., Cor., Rom.)—which are,

---

[6] *Introduction to the N. T.*, 3rd Ed., 1946, p. 248. Following Moffatt, *Introd. to the Literature of the N.T.*, 3rd Ed., 1933, p. 170.

[7] Valentinian is quoted as having spoken of substance or matter as $\varkappa \acute{\varepsilon} \nu \omega \mu \alpha$, to which the divine $\sigma o \varphi \acute{\iota} a$ had come. From this Paul is supposed to have derived his word and notion of $\varkappa \varepsilon \nu \acute{o} \omega$.

however, purely imaginary. "Language and style are unmistakably Pauline, and the Christology (2:6f.) and the Soteriology (3:6f.) show the creative power of the same spirit from which the related theses of the main Letters are derived".[8] It is in truth the same Paul and the same doctrine which we find here as for instance in Romans and Galatians.

IV

Outline and Contents

The Epistle which to such a high degree is of a personal nature and practical purport, can be divided rather precisely into two principal parts, to wit (a) 1:1—2:30 and (b) 3:1—4:23.

The contents can be more closely analysed as follows:

Introduction (1:1—11):

   (i)   Salutation (1:1, 2).

  (ii) Thanksgiving and prayer for the Church (1:3—11).

I. *Personal Circumstances of the Apostle* (1:12—26):

   (i)   Furtherance of the gospel by his imprisonment (1:12—14).

  (ii) In every way Christ is proclaimed (1:15—18).

 (iii) By life or by death Christ will be magnified (1:19—26).

II. *Kind Exhortation of the Apostle* (1:27—2:18):

   (i)   Admonition to unity, steadfastness and humility (1:27—2:4).

  (ii) Example of Christ in His Self-humiliation (2:5—11).

 (iii) Call to irreproachable conduct (2:12—18).

---

8 Feine–Behm, *Einleitung*, p. 180.

III. *Information regarding Fellow Workers* (2:19—30):
    (i)   Intention of sending Timothy to Philippi (2:19—24).
    (ii)   Epaphroditus and his return to Philippi (2:25—30).

IV. *Warning against False Teachers* (3:1—21):
    (i)   Judaistic zealots (3:1—3).
    (ii)   Carnal privileges abandoned by the apostle for the sake of Christ (3:4—11).
    (iii) Pursuit of the high calling in Christ Jesus (3:12—16).
    (iv) Enemies of the cross of Christ (3:17—19).
    (v)   The believers' glorious expectation (3:20—21).

V. *Exhortation to Various Christian Virtues* (4:1—9):
    (i)   Steadfastness and unanimity (4:1—3).
    (ii)   Joy and forbearance (4:4—5).
    (iii) Freedom from anxiety (4:6—7).
    (iv) Other virtues (4:8—9).

VI. *Grateful Recognition of Gifts Received* (4:10—20):
    (i)   Contentment under all circumstances (4:10—13).
    (ii)   Appreciation of the Church's helpfulness (4:14—18).
    (iii) God's sufficiency for every need (4:19—20).

Conclusion (4:21—23):
    Greetings and benediction (4:21—23).

V

The Unity of the Epistle

On account of the noticeable change in the theme and tone of the apostle in ch. 3:1(b), where he attacks the Judaistic teachers,[9] the original unity of the Letter is questioned in some quarters. It is asserted that a portion of another letter by Paul was inserted here.[10]

Of such a division in the Letter, at this point, however, we have no manuscript evidence at all. The contents of the first and second halves of Philippians, on the contrary, form a whole: 4:10f. refers to and is connected with 2:25f. and both treat of the Church's gift to the apostle. And the change in tone and theme after 3:1 can be explained simply as a deliberate interruption in the apostle's theme and trend of thought, because other matters (e.g. the danger of the Judaizers) gave him occasion to write about them also, and the subsequent entirely different theme demanded another tone from that of the former part of the Letter.[11] A similar sudden change in language and tone we likewise find in 2 Cor. 10—13, without being thereby compelled to abandon the idea of the unity of the Letter.

The possibility that Paul could actually have written several letters to the Philippians is suggested by (a) the expression τὰ αὐτὰ γράφειν *(to write the same things)* in 3:1; (b) the expression in Polycarp's Letter to the Philippians that the apostle ἀπὼν ὑμῖν ἔγραψεν ἐπιστολάς *(being absent wrote letters to you);* and (c) the mention of two Letters to the Philippians in the Syrian canon towards the end of the fourth century.

---

9 "From a grateful and admonitory tone in 1:1—3:1 to a sharp combative one at 3:2ff." (Thiessen, *Introduction,* p. 248).

10 Thus C. Clemen, J. Weiss, Hausrath, McNeile, Lake and others. Among them there is a marked difference as to the extent of the supposed interpolation—whether it extends to 3:19, to 4:1 or to 4:3.

11 Cf. Clogg, *Introd. to the N. T.,* 1937, p. 106f. Also Feine–Behm, *Einleitung,* p. 180f.

These arguments, however, do not carry sufficient weight to establish the existence of still another Letter to the Philippians, which was either incorporated in the one known to us or got lost. (a) The expression "to write the same things" (3:1) need not refer to a former writing to the Philippians, but can mean that he writes once more about what he referred to earlier in his Letter, or that he now writes to them about what he formerly mentioned orally on one of his visits (see exposition of the verse). (b) The word ἐπιστολάς (letters) in the epistle of Polycarp need not necessarily be taken in the plural sense because the grammatical plural form can also have a singular meaning here—as Lat. *literae*—and simply mean "letter".[12] (c) As to the Syrian canon, the first mention in it of a letter to the Philippians is to be taken as a slip of the pen, and Ephesus is evidently meant, as can be deduced from the length of the Epistle— indicated by the number of its textual divisions.[13]

VI

Character and General Theme

The Letter is presented as being written for personal reasons without dogmatic intention or polemic inclination. The frank and hearty tone, the artless form, the cheerful mood even under oppressive circumstances, the practical purport—these all bear a very personal stamp, and make

---

[12] Cf. Lightfoot, *Comm. on Philippians*, on 3:1, and his remarks on "Lost Epistles to the Philippians?" (pp. 138-142). Also Moffatt, *Introduction*, p. 173.

[13] Cf. Feine–Behm, *Einleitung*, p. 180.

it—to a measure surpassing any other letter of the apostle—*a letter,* the effusion of the heart to a Church he loved.[14]

The leading thought of the Letter, which is cordial and sincere, is: joy and gratitude. Bengel put it thus: *Summa epistolae: gaudeo, gaudete.* The word "rejoice" or other words of similar meaning, appears sixteen times in this short Letter. Even the imprisonment or malicious action of opponents could not extinguish his joy in the Lord (cf. 1:18; 2:2; 3:1; 4:1; 4:4).

Although the Letter is throughout practical and paranetical in its tone and character, it is nevertheless important even from the dogmatic point of view. Phil. 2:5—11 is the *locus classicus* for the doctrine of the pre-existence of Christ and His twofold state of humiliation and exaltation. Phil. 2:7 is the *sedes doctrinae* for the so-called kenosis theory. Other Pauline doctrines are also mentioned in the Epistle: justification by faith (3:9), the *unio mystica* (3:10, 4:13), and the expectation of the parousia (1:6; 2:10, 11; 3:20, 21; 4:5b).

VII

Time and Place of Origin

Philippians is one of the four so-called Imprisonment Letters. That Paul was in captivity on account of and in consequence of his work as apostle among the heathen appears more than once in the Letter. References to his imprisonment appear in 1:7; 1:13, 14; 2:17. In order to fix the time and place of the origin of this Letter one must

---

14 Bratt (*New Testament Guide,* 1946, p. 66), on account of its exhortations and its words of praise on the advance of the gospel, calls it "a spiritual tonic, fitted to brace one up when he is low in spirits."

determine the imprisonment during which the apostle wrote this Letter.

According to the Acts of the Apostles Paul was a prisoner at Philippi (16:23), Jerusalem (21:33f.), Caesarea (23:25) and Rome (28:16). His imprisonments at Philippi and at Jerusalem, however, were of very short duration—one or two days—and the named cities cannot therefore be considered as places from which the apostle would have written Letters. Seeing that it appears from texts like 2 Cor. 6:5 and 11:23, 24 (written towards the end of the third missionary journey) that there were more imprisonments (as well as other serious hardships) than those of which the Acts of the Apostles makes mention, Ephesus has also been proposed as a possible place of imprisonment from which one or more Letters could have been written.[15]

The choice of the place of origin, therefore, lies between Caesarea, Ephesus and Rome, and the time of composition will have to be fixed accordingly.

In favour of Caesarea[16] the following is adduced:

(a) The imprisonment (lit. "bonds") of which Phil. 1:13 makes mention, is better understood of Paul's circumstances in Caesarea under military custody than of those in Rome where he was fairly free to move about and to preach

---

[15] For the different views regarding the place of origin of the Imprisonment Letters: J. Schmid, *Zeit und Ort der Paulinischen Gefangenschaftsbriefe*, 1931.

[16] Although there are quite a number of theologians who regard the other Imprisonment Letters (Col., Philem. and Eph.) as written from Caesarea, but who exclude Philippians, there are nevertheless still some among the later set who regard Philippians also as written at Caesarea. Among them especially O. Holtzmann, Spitta and Lohmeyer deserve mention.

(Acts 28:30, 31). Over against this, however, it could be asserted that Paul undoubtedly, as the legal process was nearing its end following the two years of which Acts 28 makes mention, would have been subjected to stricter custody, of which this Letter gives evidence, and that the former *custodia libera* gave way to the *custodia militaris.*

(b) The praetorium (Phil. 1:13) must be identified with the Palace of Herod at Caesarea, of which Acts 23:35 makes mention, while "Caesar's household" (Phil. 4:22) can refer to dependents of Caesar's household or slaves who were elsewhere than at Rome (in this case also at Caesarea). To this, however, it may be answered that according to Phil. 1:13 Paul's bonds became known "throughout the whole praetorium *and to all the rest,*" and that by this last addition the praetorium is qualified as *Caesar's guard* (9,000 strong) *in Rome,* and could not mean only Caesar's *palace.* The word here has personal content and in this sense could be used only in connection with Rome. In like manner it is the most natural explanation to take "Caesar's household" (4:22) to be the household at the imperial court of Rome. There is no conclusive proof to be found that elsewhere there were such dependents of the imperial household as at Rome and that they could lay claim to the appellation "Caesar's household" with as much right as those at Rome.

(c) The sharp controversy in Phil. 3 is directed against the Jews, the instigators of the agitation against Paul in Jerusalem (Acts 21:27), and can be understood as directed against them from Caesarea immediately after Paul had been taken thence under military escort. Against this, however, the argument can be launched that Phil. 3 is not directed against the Jews, but against the Judaizers in Christian circles. Compare the general traits thereof:

23

Phil. 3:2 with 2 Cor. 11:13 and Gal. 5:12; Phil. 3:3 with Gal. 6:13; Phil. 3:5 with 2 Cor. 11:22.

Further objections can be launched against Caesarea as the place of imprisonment where the Letter was written. Acts 23—26 hardly allows for such extensive labour in the gospel at Caesarea during Paul's imprisonment there as is apparent from Phil. 1:12—18 (cf. also Col. 4:2—4, Eph. 6:18—20). Furthermore it is striking that no mention whatsoever is made of the evangelist Philip who lived at Caesarea and in whose house Paul enjoyed hospitality shortly before his imprisonment (Acts 21:8). Finally Paul's peculiar frame of mind at a time when he was confronted with the possibility of a martyrdom (as is apparent from Phil. 1:20—25, 2:17), does not fit in with the imprisonment at Caesarea, from where he could always still appeal to the Emperor at Rome, as he eventually actually did under Festus.

In favour of Ephesus[17] as the place of imprisonment which is presupposed in the Letter, the following is adduced:

(a) Paul makes mention in 2 Cor. 11:23 of imprisonments (plural) which he had to endure for the sake of the gospel. In the reports of the Acts relating to the period up to the time of writing 2 Corinthians (viz. in Macedonia at the end of the third missionary journey, after a sojourn of three years at Ephesus), only a short imprisonment at Philippi is mentioned (Acts 16:24). There must, therefore, have been other imprisonments of which Luke made no

---

[17] Among the supporters of the Ephesus hypothesis the following can be mentioned: Deissmann, Appel, Lake, Feine–Behm, Duncan, Manson, McNeile, Goguel, Obbink–Brouwer and Michaelis. Cf. for an enumeration of the reasons for their point of view: Greijdanus, *Bijzondere Canoniek*, II, 1949, p. 131f.

mention. At Ephesus there was most probably such an imprisonment, from where Paul accordingly could have sent the Letter. It is all the more likely because 1 Cor. 15:31, 32 (written at Ephesus) states that Paul, humanly speaking, fought at Ephesus with wild beasts; and 2 Cor. 1:8, 9 makes mention of "affliction" which Paul experienced in Asia (Ephesus?) so that he even "despaired of life itself," and "had even received the sentence of death."

These (and other) arguments in favour of the Ephesus hypothesis would surely have a certain amount of cogency if independently thereof it was certain that the apostle had actually been a prisoner at Ephesus. But there is—notwithstanding 2 Cor. 11:23—no direct proof resting on available sources, that Paul suffered imprisonment at Ephesus. In Acts 19 Luke mentions Paul's sojourn of three years at Ephesus and the riot headed by Demetrius, but nothing of an imprisonment;[18] and in none of his Letters does Paul himself expressly mention any such experience there. Even from 1 Cor. 15:31, 32 and 2 Cor. 1:8, 9 no such proof can be deduced. As a Roman citizen Paul could neither be thrown to the wild beasts nor could he be sentenced to fight against them, so that 1 Cor. 15:32 must not be taken in a literal sense but figuratively. Deadly perils (as appears from 2 Cor. 1:10) still threatened Paul even in Macedonia, after he had already departed from Asia, so that 2 Cor. 1:9, 10 probably is to be taken to mean conspiracies of such a nature as that mentioned in Acts 20:3.

(b) Phil. 2:25—30 presupposes close contact between

---

[18] Michaelis, himself an advocate of this view, acknowledges: "Als eine Schwierigkeit musz es zweifellos gelten, dass wir aus Apg. 19 nichts über eine Ephesische Gefangenschaft des Paulus erfahren" (*Einleitung in das N. T.*, 1946, p. 209).

the Church at Philippi and the imprisoned apostle, and one may presume that no great distance separated them from one another. Ephesus fits well in this picture because communications could take place easily and fairly regularly. Over against this one may remark that although Philippi was situated nearer to Ephesus than to Rome, there also was much intercourse between Philippi and Rome, and that the few years of imprisonment were more than enough for oral or written communications and missions between Philippi and Rome, especially if we bear in mind the fact that the Letter is to be regarded as the last of the four Imprisonment Letters.

(c)   The Letter to the Philippians belongs, as far as its theological ideas and language are concerned, to the earlier and great Letters of Paul (Thess., Gal., Cor., Rom.), and must have originated about the same time they were written, probably on the third missionary journey. Resemblance in ideas between Letters does, however, not yet prove that they have their origin in the same time or circumstances; much rather the circumstances of each Church to which a Letter was written determined the manner of the writing. Philippians need for that reason, therefore, not be classified and dated with the older dogmatic or apologetic writings.

Finally we can merely add that the significant expressions "praetorian guard" (Phil. 1:13) and "Caesar's household" (Phil. 4:22) favour Ephesus no more than Caesarea.

In favour of Rome[19] as the place of imprisonment whence

---

[19]   Advocates of this view constitute the huge majority of theologians and students of Scripture. Up to the 18th century it was the only and general view held on this matter. Among the later names are to be mentioned: B. Weiss, Zahn, Haupt, Ewald, Jülicher, Moffatt, Baljon, Kennedy, Vincent, Lightfoot, Barth, Greijdanus, Thiessen.

the Letter was written—a view held by the great majority of students of Scripture—the following arguments are brought forward:

(a)   Acts 28:16, 30, 31 makes mention of Paul's imprisonment at Rome for two years, pending his trial as a result of his appeal to Caesar.

(b)   The whole tradition of the early Church pleads for Rome and for the dating of the Imprisonment Letters as written at Rome, and this remained undisputed up to the eighteenth century. (In 1731 Oeder proposed Corinth as the place of origin of Philippians, and since 1799 Caesarea has been suggested—first by H. E. G. Paulus—,while only as recently as 1900—by Lisco—Ephesus was put forward as the place of origin of the Imprisonment Letters).

(c)   The expressions "praetorian guard" (Phil. 1:13) and "Caesar's household" (Phil. 4:22) are decisively in favour of Rome. For it was there where the praetorian guard, a force of 9,000 men, was stationed, among whom in the course of years the reason of Paul's imprisonment—that his bonds were "in Christ"—became known, in contrast with Caesarea or Ephesus where the reason for arrest would have become known immediately, so that everybody would have known it very soon. And it was there also in the first instance where those belonging to the household of Caesar were to be found in large numbers.

(d)   Paul's mention of the great number of preachers who were working in that city, some as kindly disposed fellow workers and others hostile to him (Phil. 1:14—18), suits Rome best.

(e)   Finally Paul's reference to his imprisonment and the progress of the case as "a defence and confirmation of the gospel" (Phil. 1:7) decides in favour of Rome, for from this can be adduced that the process was nearing its end, and that Paul was facing the judicial decision of either the sentence of death or acquittal (Phil. 1:19, 20; 2:17). Paul had already appeared before the tribunal, the case had already begun (1:7—12), and it was already known to all that the prisoner was there as a missionary of Christianity (1:12f.). Compared with Acts 28:16, 30, 31 the Letter depicts a changed and advanced stage of his captivity: Paul is no longer in his own hired house with liberty to preach and unlimited intercourse with others; he is under military custody and probably has been transferred to the prisoner's ward under close guard. The final decision is imminent. And such an imperial judgment where the last decision is made, can only take place in Rome.[20]

We, therefore, come to the conclusion that the Letter to the Philippians was written during the (first) imprisonment of Paul at Rome (60 A.D. and later), and, more exactly, after the two years of which Acts 28 makes mention, thus 62—63 A.D.

---

[20] Compare Clogg's conclusion: "Cumulative evidence may seem to favour Ephesus ... but it does not amount to proof ... The balance of evidence supports Rome, the traditional place of writing of the other three Captivity Letters" (*Introduction*, p. 80).

EXPOSITION

THE EPISTLE OF PAUL TO THE PHILIPPIANS

EXPOSITION

CHAPTER I

SALUTATION

1:1, 2

1 Paul and Timothy, servants of Christ Jesus, to all the saints in Christ Jesus that are at Philippi, with the bishops and deacons:

2 Grace to you and peace from God our Father and the Lord Jesus Christ.

1 This most personal of all letters of Paul—as it is sometimes styled—begins in an unaffected and hearty way, with the customary mention of its senders.[1] With the exception of the Letter to the Ephesians, the names of Paul and Timothy are mentioned together in all the so-called Imprisonment Letters as being the senders, which serves as an indication of the close association and intimate fellowship of these two ambassadors of Christ, even at Rome.[2]

---

[1] All thirteen Pauline Letters begin by stating the name of the writer or sender. A comparison of the N. T. Letters with the private correspondence of the contemporaries of the apostle, indicates that in more than one respect Paul makes use of the customary polite letter-phraseology which was common among the middle classes of those times. First of all there usually is the opening salutation, which makes mention of the writer of the letter, followed by thanksgiving or prayer for the person(s) to whom it is written, and after that the special message or matter or contents to be communicated, while the whole is concluded with a benediction or prayer. As appears from the papyri, the whole framework of the Pauline Letters is typical of his times. Cf. C. M. Cobern, *The New Archaeological Discoveries and their bearing upon the New Testament,* 1917, pp. 582—590.

[2] Their names are mentioned together as the senders of four earlier Letters, viz. those to Corinth and those to Thessalonica, as well as three of the Imprisonment Letters (Philippians, Colossians and Philemon).

Timothy was no stranger at Philippi. Together with Paul on his second missionary journey he participated in the foundation of the Church at Philippi with all the significant incidents experienced on that occasion (cf. Acts 16:3, 17:14f. and Phil. 2:22); afterwards he once again visited the churches of Macedonia (of which Philippi was the capital) (Acts 19:22; 20:3, 4), and before long he would be commissioned by Paul to go there again (Phil. 2:19—23).

Although Timothy is mentioned in the salutation as fellow sender, it appears from what follows later on, that Paul holds himself alone responsible as the real author of the contents of the letter.[3] It is, however, quite possible—even probable—that Timothy acted as secretary or amanuensis to Paul in the writing of the letter.[4]

"Servants (slaves) of Christ Jesus"[5] the writers call them-

---

[3] Except in the salutation, the writer speaks throughout in the first person, singular, as "I" (1:3, 12, 13, 14, 16; 2:2, 12; 3:1; 4:1 etc.) and Timothy is mentioned in the third person and quite objectively in 2:19—23.

[4] That Paul employed an amanuensis or secretary to whom he, according to the custom of his day, dictated his Letters, is apparent from Rom. 16:22, where the name of the amanuensis of that Letter is given (just as that of Peter's in 1 Petr. 5:12), and also from the indications that he added something in his own hand at the conclusion of his dictated Letters, cf. 2 Thess. 3:17, Gal. 6:11, 1 Cor. 16:21—24, Col. 4:18. See also Cobern, *New Archaeological Discoveries*, p. 584.

[5] The sequence in which the names of the Lord are given here (as *Jesus Christ* in some Mss. and as *Christ Jesus* in others, as also in the phrase immediately following), is of no great importance. Paul uses both sequences alternately—the former in 1:11 and 2:11, and the latter in 1:26 and 2:5, whilst he more often only uses the name *Christ* (1:10, 15, 18, etc.), and once only the name *Jesus* (2:10).

If the sequence *Christ Jesus* is the correct one here—by reason of the stronger Mss. evidence in favour of it—the emphasis falls in the

selves. This title by which they indicate themselves is unusual, especially since it is used without any reference to the apostleship of Paul which distinguishes him from Timothy as, for instance, is the case in the preamble to the Letter to the Colossians (Col. 1:1). The fact, however, that Paul does not make any mention here of his apostleship, as in most of his other Letters[6] (and as was quite necessary in the case of Colossae, as he was not the founder of that church), can be readily explained. On the one hand because of his personal acquaintance with the people at Philippi and the confidential nature of his letter, no further introduction to his official capacity as apostle was required. And on the other hand there was evidently none at Philippi who questioned his apostolic authority.

Both Paul and Timothy are called servants of Jesus Christ. However much they differed from each other in other respects—in years, in the circumstances of their conversion, in spiritual maturity (Timothy was Paul's "spiritual child" and probably a convert at Lystra on his first missionary journey), in official activity (apostle and evangelist respectively)—yet in Christ they were equals; both were slaves of Christ, with the same calling, the same ministry of the gospel, the same Master. "Servants of Christ Jesus" is a general term here for the workers of the Lord, His ambassadors and messengers, and indicates their entire identification with Christ and His cause on earth, as well as their unconditional and dutiful service to Him as their Lord (Master), who exercised the right of possession

---

first instance on His official name *Christ*, the Anointed, and only afterwards on the proper name or personal name *Jesus*, in His historical appearance.

6 Cf. Rom. 1:1, 1 Cor. 1:1, 2 Cor. 1:1, Gal. 1:1, Eph. 1:1, etc.

and disposal over them, and on Whom they were
entirely dependent and to Whom alone they were responsible. This lowly and humble self-appellation, furthermore,
is a renunciation of all self-importance and self-esteem, and
so the light is focused more intensely on Him Who alone
is their Lord, "to Whom they belong and Whom they
serve."

The letter is addressed "to all the saints in Christ Jesus,"[7]
and not only to individual believers in the church, although
later on special mention is made of the bishops and deacons,
the officials of the church. On several occasions in the letter
Paul's thoughts are drawn to all in the Church (cf. 1:4, 7, 8,
25 etc.), to indicate therewith the apostle's interest in and
his attachment to the church as a whole and its members
individually. To him the church was a unity from which
he excluded nobody.

The members of the church are called "saints" (holy ones)
in Christ Jesus. Saintliness or holiness must not be taken
here subjectively as an innate ethical quality attached to
the believers, an inward purity, or devotion to God, which
is *in them* (although ideally and in principle it is the part
of every believer), but must be understood in an objective
sense, in inseparable connection with "in Christ Jesus,"
as a being sanctified *in Him*. In themselves the believers are
not yet holy; only in Christ, considered in the light of His
righteousness, as set apart for Him, and liberated by Him
and in His blood and through His Spirit, they are holy.
Although they are called to holiness and have to strive after

---

[7] For a corresponding title in other Letters of Paul, cf. Rom. 1:7
(Beloved of God, called to be saints), Col. 1:2 (Saints and faithful
brethren in Christ), and especially 1 Cor. 1:2 (Consecrated in Christ
Jesus, called to be saints).

it, and there is taking place in believers a continual process of inward transformation and sanctification in Christ, yet holiness describes, in its primary sense, the state or position in which they are placed in Christ. "Holy people are 'unholy people' who are, however, set apart by God as such and who are claimed and taken into possession for His dominion, for His use, for Him Who is holy. In Christ Jesus is and abides their holiness. In Him they are holy; only in connection with Him can they be so called, and in no other respect" (Barth).

Among the saints at Philippi the officials, the bishops and deacons,[8] enjoy special mention. They held positions of special responsibility and performed special services, also to Paul,[9] which entitled them to be particularly mentioned next to the church in general. They were people appointed by the church to perform definite functions: the bishops were specially charged to lead and govern and supervise the church (as official title the term presbyter or elder was also used), while the deacons "served the tables" and had to perform the duties of Christian charity (cf. Acts 6:1—6, 14:23, 1 Tim. 3:1-13). So both had a share in the spiritual care of the church.

2 The salutation is at the same time a prayer for the church. The word "grace" in the original contains an allusion to the usual Greek way of greeting,[10] but fills it with a true

---

[8] This verse is one of the oldest evidences for the existence in the early Christian churches of both the offices mentioned.

[9] Not only on previous occasions, but also with regard to the recent collection and dispatch of financial support to him during his imprisonment at Rome (Phil. 4:15, 16 and 4:10, 18).

[10] The general Greek greeting χαίρειν also appears in Scripture, e.g. in Acts 15:23; 23:26, James 1:1. For the use of the word in the

and new Christian content. The word "grace" comes to include all the deeds of God, in which the free, undeserved favour of God towards the sinner finds expression. To the prayer for grace[11] Paul adds that for peace, the characteristic Hebrew salutation which does not only indicate here the inner peace of mind and composure, but also gives expression once more to the particular Christian idea of peace with God, reconciliation with God, on which the peace of the heart, the inward joy of mind and the peace with the fellow man is rooted. In this "Greek and Jewish greeting deepened in a Christian sense" (Greijdanus) we have a comprehensive expression for all that is essential and indispensable in the Christian religion—a salutation which comprises the whole message of the Gospel—a prayer in which is revealed that the grace and the peace of God are the first and the last and the best which we can petition from God for one another.

The blessings of grace and peace have their origin in God himself as the Source of all perfection and good gifts. There is no grace except in God, and no real peace except that which flows from God reconciled with the sinner.

The fatherhood of God also, with its associations of tender mercy and love and provision for His children, is closely linked here with the mention of God. Moreover, a declaration of personal faith does not remain in abeyance, but finds expression in the words: "God our Father", which accentuates the privilege, common to both writer and reader, of being a child of God.

N. T. in different meanings and on different occasions, vide Abbott–Smith, *Manual Greek Lexicon of the N. T.*, p. 477ff., and Cremer, *Biblico-Theological Lexicon of the N. T. Greek*, p. 572.

11 This prayer for grace (and peace) appears in all Paul's Letters, while in the two Letters to Timothy mercy is also added.

The "Lord Jesus Christ" is named together with the Father as the source of grace and peace. This title brings forward His glorious Name as Mediator, whereby He is indicated as Lord (as the Exalted He is the *Kyrios* or Lord), as Redeemer (the historic Jesus), and as Messiah (Christ, meaning the Anointed). From God the Father the richest blessings flow to the Church, by virtue of the mediatorial work and atoning sacrifice of His Son Jesus Christ.

1:3—8

3 I thank my God upon all my remembrance of you,

4 always in every supplication of mine on behalf of you all
making my supplication with joy,

5 for your fellowship in furtherance of the gospel from the
first day until now;

6 being confident of this very thing, that he who began a
good work in you will perfect it until the day of Jesus
Christ:

7 even as it is right for me to be thus minded on behalf of
you all, because I have you in my heart, inasmuch as, both
in my bonds and in the defence and confirmation of the
gospel, ye all are partakers with me of grace.

8 For God is my witness, how I long after you all in the
tender mercies of Christ Jesus.

3 In all his Letters to the churches, excepting one (viz.
Galatians), Paul begins with thanksgiving and praise. There
is always reason to praise God, there are always circumstances which induce gratitude, even where otherwise
warnings and rebukes are to be meted out to the church.
So far as Philippi is concerned, Paul renders thanks to God[1]
especially for their partnership in the gospel in more than

---

[1] The reading *I thank my God* is in some Mss. rendered by:
I, however, thank our Lord. Though the latter reading is preferred
by some exegetes (e.g. Ewald, Zahn, Moffatt, K. Barth), it not only
has poorer manuscript support, and differs altogether from the usual
Pauline expression in other Letters (cf. 1 Cor. 1:4; Col. 1:3; 1 Thess.
1:2), but therein a contrast is assumed between Paul and either
Timothy or the church at Philippi, which nowhere appears in the
Letter.

one way, which was a token of the grace which the church received.

If the apostle gives thanks to "my God," he thereby gives evidence of the most personal and close alliance of faith with God (as also in Rom. 1:8 and Philemon 4), which is at the same time his testimony given to his readers, a confession which revives in his memory such experiences as his conversion, his calling, his service for Christ—all the outstanding occasions on which God made Himself known to him as *his* God in a very special way, as that God "to Whom he belongs and Whom he also serves" (Acts 27:23).

This thanksgiving is rendered "upon all my remembrance of you,"[2] i.e. "every time I think of you," and therefore points to a lovely relation and disposition of the church towards him since its foundation and also afterwards, a lasting fellowship in the gospel.

4 Seeing that the reason for his thanksgiving is not stated until verse 5, this verse is to be regarded as a parenthesis, an insertion standing by itself. Literally we have here: "Always in every supplication[3] of mine for you all with joy

---

[2] The idea of $\dot{v}\mu\tilde{\omega}v$ as subjective genitive should be rejected together with the resultant meaning of the sentence: "I thank my God for all your remembrance of me." For (a) elsewhere in the Pauline Letters the objective genitive follows after $\mu\nu\varepsilon\dot{\iota}a$ (Rom. 1:9; Eph. 1:16); (b) the omission of μov as obj. gen. in the sentence would be more difficult to explain than its omission as subj. gen. in the sense in which we understand the verse; (c) Paul is not *only* moved to thanksgiving by their remembrance (and gifts) of him, but especially by their partnership in the gospel. He thanks God, therefore, *in his remembrance of them*, whenever he thinks of them.

[3] $\delta\acute{\varepsilon}\eta\sigma\iota\varsigma$ differs from the more usual $\pi\varrho\sigma\varepsilon v\chi\acute{\eta}$ in that the latter is the ordinary word used for prayer, while the former more definitely

making entreaty." Next to thanksgiving it always remains necessary to render intercession, supplication, prayer to God for the church. For there is always still need, spiritual want, imperfection (cf. verses 9, 10). Prayer for the church is furthermore accompanied by joy. With emphasis it is stated that Paul constantly at every approach to God intercedes for the church, that he prays to God on behalf of them all, and that each such occasion and labour in prayer on behalf of them is a matter of joy to him. Gratitude and joy accompany every thought of Paul in his prayer-closet, when remembering the church at Philippi.

5 Now the occasion for or object of thanksgiving is definitely stated,[4] viz. their "partnership in the gospel" (RSV). Their share or partnership in (or towards) the gospel was not a quiet enjoyment of it, but a keen activity in the interest of it,[5] an effective participation for the furtherance of the gospel, "from the first day until now," from the first time it was first preached to them by Paul (Acts 16:13ff.) until now. That fellowship of the church in the gospel reveals

---

denotes entreaty or supplication. Cf. Cremer, p. 174, and Kittel II, pp. 40 and 806.

4 That this verse follows after verse 3 as object of εὐχαριστῶ (and that verse 4 should be read as a parenthesis), is clear, among other considerations, from the following: (a) εὐχαριστῶ would otherwise have no object; (b) "the fellowship in furtherance of the gospel" is not the subject of Paul's entreaty (verse 4), but of his thanksgiving (verse 3); (c) the preposition ἐπί is used by Paul with verbs like εὐχαριστεῖν (cf. 1 Cor. 1:4; 2 Cor. 9:15), but not with δέησιν ποιεῖν or δεῖσθαι, to mark its cause or ground. (Cf. Vincent, I.C.C. ad loc.).

5 Here a less common construction is used after κοινωνία, viz. εἰς with the accusative, in which is included the idea of motion, direction, a striving towards.

different aspects: their acceptance of the gospel in faith, their identification with the aims thereof, their co-operation in preaching and spreading it, their expression of sympathy with the apostle in his afflictions for the sake of Christ (verse 7), amongst others, by sending pecuniary contributions for the relief of his needs in prison (Phil. 4:14—17) or for the benefit of other fellow believers by collecting for them (Rom. 15:26). In short, it refers to their sympathetic attitude and practical action in the interest of the gospel: their co-operation, zeal, prayers and sacrifice, arising from their personal appropriation of the gospel by faith.[6]

6 Paul's trust in God for the continuation of the fellowship in the gospel, is another reason for his thanksgiving and joy. That confidence is not vested in the Philippians and in their steadfastness or irreproachable past, but in God,[7] Who began, and Who also brings to completion, and who never forsakes the works of His hands.

He who began the good work among them at Philippi, was not Paul, and not even the Philippians themselves by their conversion, but God.[8] It was indeed "God who worketh in you both to will and to work, for his good pleasure" (2:13). It is a work of grace that is meant here, which can only be the fruit of divine action. "A good work" undoubtedly has a wider meaning than the previously

---

[6] Cf. E. P. Groenewald, *Κοινωνία by Paulus*, 1932, p. 135.

[7] By virtue of the position of the words, particular stress is laid on αὐτὸ τοῦτο. This accusative after πεποιθώς is unusual—the verb being usually followed by a preposition—but the same construction is found again in verse 25. A fuller description of αὐτὸ τοῦτο follows after it, introduced by ὅτι.

[8] A similar omission of θεός in the text, as we have here, can also be noted in Rom. 8:11, Gal. 1:16, 1 Thess. 5:24.

mentioned partnership in the gospel, and denotes a more comprehensive work of grace in the hearts of the believers, affecting both the inner disposition and the outward activity,—a union of faith with Christ as well as an activity of faith for His cause.

This work of grace—which has to grow, progress and come to perfection (cf. 3:12)—will be brought to completion by God. This also will not be the fruit of human exertion, but the full-grown fruit of God's grace. The "good work" in them will reach its culmination and perfection not on the day of the death of the believers and their departure from this world, but at "the day of Christ", i.e. the day of His Advent, the day of His revelation as the Judge of heaven and earth, the day of His final victory. For that day of judgment the church must prepare itself, and up to that day the sanctification of the bridal church, and also her partnership in the gospel, must be continued (cf. 1 Thess. 5:23). Not before that day will the church reach its ultimate destination,[9] will the redemptive work of Christ come to completion.

7 It is only fair that the apostle should feel thus about the church (cherish such a disposition towards them); love for them and knowledge of them impose this obligation on him, for he holds them in his heart,[10] i.e. he knows them in

---

[9] The work of salvation in believers is, therefore, not regarded as atomistic or individual. Each brick in the wall only then attains its destination and goal, and fulfils its purpose, when the whole building has been completed and is dedicated.

[10] "Have ... in my heart" can mean: to love or to know. According to the context the heart is to be taken not primarily as "seat of affection" but as "seat of reflection" (M. Jones, *Westminster Comm. ad loc.*)

loving thoughts as partakers of his grace, both in his imprisonment, and in the defense of the gospel.

Paul was in prison, in bonds,[11] and as prisoner he was
called to defend the gospel before the judge at his trial. As
its advocate, he maintained and vindicated the Gospel truth
before the tribunal,[12] and thereby he not only confirmed
it, but it also found wider acceptance. The faith of the
believers was strengthened, and also outsiders became con-
vinced of the truth thereof. With regard to this the
apostle calls the church "partakers with me of grace" (better:
my partakers of grace). This not only expresses a common
experience of those redeemed by the saving grace of God in
Christ, but (taken in connection with their "partnership in
the gospel", verse 5) also means that the church has a share
in the affliction and suffering for the cause of the gospel as
well as in its defence and confirmation, by their sympathy
with and support of Paul—by identifying themselves with
him and his cause at Rome. It is God-given grace to labour
for Christ, and it is grace also to be allowed to suffer for
Christ (cf. 1:29). By their sharing with Paul in his suffering
and labour, they gave evidence that they were also partakers
with him of the grace of God.

8 As Paul cannot find words to give expression to his
longing for them, he appeals to the fact that God who judges

---

[11] "Bonds" describes the imprisonment of the apostle. It may
denote captivity in general, without a closer description of the nature
of it (cf. verse 14), or may be taken in the literal sense of chains
(cf. Col. 4:18, Eph. 6:20).

[12] Paul's attitude in the first instance is one of defence, not of
himself or his life, but of the gospel of which he has become a preacher.
It therefore not so much concerns himself, but the cause of his Master.
This is all that counts with the apostle.

the hearts of men, knows how tenderly and sincerely he is attached to them, how he "holds them in his heart," how his affection for them grows into a great yearning for them. At the same time it is not so much the intensity of his love and yearning, but the distinctive nature of it, to which Paul gives expression by adding the phrase "in the tender mercies[13] of Christ Jesus." It is more than human love, it is spiritual attachment in Christ. "With the heart of Christ Jesus" the apostle is yearning for the church; it is Christ Himself Who in and through Paul loves them and longs for them; for in a deep mystical sense Christ Himself lives in him (Gal. 2:20) and loves through him.[14]

---

[13] σπλάγχνα literally means: intestines, the inner parts, being the seat of the affections, in the same sense in which we generally speak of the heart. Metaphorically, the word is used to denote the inner feelings of love, pity, tenderness.

[14] "The believer has no yearnings apart from his Lord; his pulse beats with the pulse of Christ; his heart throbs with the heart of Christ" (J. B. Lightfoot, Comm. *ad loc.*).

1:9—11

9 And this I pray, that your love may abound yet more and more in knowledge and all discernment;

10 so that ye may approve the things that are excellent; that ye may be sincere and void of offence unto the day of Christ;

11 being filled with the fruits of righteousness, which are through Jesus Christ, unto the glory and praise of God.

9 Gratitude towards God for the church's partnership in the gospel not only rouses the apostle's yearning for them, but also urges him to intercede for them.[1] His thoughts regarding them complete themselves in intercession to God for their further sanctification and perfection, that their love may abound more and more with knowledge and all discernment. Love is already experienced —love towards God and Christ, as well as love towards the apostle and mutual love towards each other as partakers of grace (verse 7). But this love is as yet imperfect and must abound more and more, especially in depth and quality, viz. in advanced knowledge[2] (knowledge of God) and in all discernment,[3] spiritual judgment and moral discrimination.

---

[1] By the emphatic position of τοῦτο the attention is deliberately drawn to what follows, the contents and purport of the prayer.

[2] ἐπίγνωσις is a stronger word than γνῶσις, and denotes a deeper and more advanced knowledge. Cf. also Paul's prayer for the Colossians, "to be filled with the knowledge of His will" (1:9).

[3] The word αἴσθησις, which is used only here in the N. T., means perception, being derived from αἰσθάνομαι, and expresses the idea of discernment and judiciousness. Cf. Kittel I, p. 186.

The love of the believers must accordingly be able to know rightly and to sense clearly and to distinguish correctly; it must be an "intelligent and discriminating love" (Vincent), for it must

10 be competent to "approve[4] the things that are[5] excellent," it must be able to determine by judicious discernment what things really matter, what is the best and most virtuous, and what is of most importance. The church must not only be able to distinguish between good and evil in the religio-ethical domain, but must be able to determine what is really of value; it must be able to discriminate and to judge with a deep spiritual insight as to the nature and value of things. Where this is the case, the church will be "sincere[6] and void of offence"; the believers will, as far as they themselves are concerned, lead an inwardly pure and clean and unpolluted life, while their conduct towards others will be blameless, without giving offence or being a stumbling-block to others. A pure inner disposition will result in a blameless outward conduct of life (cf. Rom. 14:13). Such an attitude is demanded of the church with a view to[7] and mindful of the day of Christ, the day of His

---

[4] δοκιμάζειν is used in classical Greek to denote the assaying of coin or metal; it is also used in the sense of a crucial test; while the general meaning has come to be: to examine or test, or to approve that which has stood the test.

[5] The verb διαφέρειν can mean *differ* or *surpass, excel, stand out above*. In the latter sense τὰ διαφέροντα refers to things that are real, that count, that surpass other things.

[6] The derivation of εἰλικρινεῖς is uncertain. It probably means "tried or tested by sunlight," with the idea that—seen against the light—it was found pure and unstained and clear.

[7] εἰς is used here and not ἄχρι (as in verse 6). It does not refer

second coming (cf. verse 6), which will be the day of judgment, the great test of the purity and blamelessness of life
(cf. Matt. 25:31 ff.), as well as the day on which the believers
will be glorified together with Christ (cf. 2 Thess. 1:10,
2 Pet. 3:10, 11, Eph. 5:27).

11 The church, however, can only be pure and irreproachable, if it is filled,[8] like a tree heavily laden, with the
fruits of righteousness, if a holy life is revealed, a life that
is right before God and adapted to His will, a life abounding
in virtues and devoted to God. This subjective righteousness of life is, however, not the result of any human effort,
but is only "through Jesus Christ," who enables the
believers to attain it as He works it in them. They who
abide in Him (and He in them) bear much fruit
(John 15:4, 5).

Such a righteousness, personally experienced, serves to
the glory and praise of God. It is the ultimate aim towards
which all Christian endeavour and all godliness is directed.
All that the apostle asks for the church in this prayer: love
which is abounding more and more in knowledge and all
discernment, a pure and blameless conduct, a righteous way
of life—all these must serve to glorify God, to tender Him
honour and praise, and to magnify the virtues of Him from
whom and through whom and to whom all things are (cf.
Matt. 5:16).

---

to the time-limit, but should be understood to mean *for, towards,* or
with a view to.

8 Literally: filled or made full (perfect passive). Generally πληροῦν
is followed by the genitive, but constructions with the accusative, as
in this case, are also found, by which the "removed object" is indicated.
See also Paul's usage elsewhere, Col. 1:9; 2 Thess. 1:11.

1:12—14

12 Now I would have you know, brethren, that the things which happened unto me have fallen out rather unto the progress of the gospel;

13 so that my bonds became manifest in Christ throughout the whole praetorian guard, and to all the rest;

14 and that most of the brethren in the Lord, being confident through my bonds, are more abundantly bold to speak the word of God without fear.

12 Paul was in prison and had probably appeared before the tribunal to justify himself. The church was worried about the issue and lived in anxious suspense and uncertainty. The apostle makes haste, however, to reassure them; the cause of the gospel suffered no harm, but was benefited by his trial in Rome. The adventures[1] which befell the apostle served rather[2] towards the advancement[3] of the gospel, than being a disadvantage (as they might have feared). Paul could gratefully report this to the "brethren," —an expression he often uses to denote the believers (cf. 3:1, 3:13, 4:1), and by which their unity and spiritual attachment in Christ as children of the same Father is given

---

1 Literally: the things with regard to me, concerning me.

2 If we translate μᾶλλον by *more* instead of by *rather*, the object of comparison is wanting; therefore the translation *rather* or *really* (RSV) is the correct one here and makes sense, by which the contrast with the suspicious fears of the church stand out clearly.

3 προκόπη is probably a military term, used to denote the progress or advance of an army that has to make its way through forests and over mountains.

prominence. In spite of all the adverse circumstances and afflictions of his captivity, it could be stated with confidence that for the cause for which the apostle suffered, there was progress and advancement. It strikes us that Paul does not speak of himself, or enlarge upon his experiences, but has in mind only the cause of the gospel of which he is a servant. Even during and in spite of his imprisonment, all is well, for the gospel is being advanced. And to him that is the only thing that matters.

13 The first way in which the gospel was advanced is evident from the fact "that it became known throughout the whole praetorian guard[4] and to all the rest that my imprisonment is for Christ" (RSV). His imprisonment and the cause of it became known. It became known that he was in Rome as a prisoner—not because of any crime he committed, but for the sake of Christ and the gospel. His bonds (imprisonment) appear clearly to stand in connection with Christ. The reason for his imprisonment, his conduct as Christian prisoner, his witness for Christ and His cause during his trial, and the acceptance which the word found amongst the hearers and bystanders, was a preaching of Christ in his captivity which served for the advancement of the gospel.

The first circle to whom his bonds in Christ became

---

4 Various renderings can be given for πραιτώριον. It can mean (a) the praetorian palace or the governor's residency (as in Matt. 27:27, Mark 15:16, Acts 23:35); (b) the barracks or camping-place of the praetorian guards; (c) the praetorian body-guard (the occupants of the barracks). The phrase following in this verse, viz. "and to all the rest," indicates that by πραιτώριον here persons are meant, and not a palace or barracks. The whole praetorian guard consisted of 9 cohorts of 1,000 men each. The watch over the prisoners was entrusted to the guard, who took over the duty by turns and alternately.

manifest, was the "whole praetorian guard," of whom a large number came in personal contact with the apostle during the years of his captivity, because the guards watching the prisoner constantly relieved each other and so the members of the praetorian guard all became informed of the reason for Paul's imprisonment. They were the nearest circle around Paul; and to them, but also to "all the rest," this information was conferred. The "rest" denotes a wider circle in Rome who were interested in his imprisonment and trial, and eventually became acquainted with everything in connection with him. Among them must be reckoned all those to whom Acts 28:17, 23, 30 refer, although Paul here does not designate them more closely.

14 In the second instance the gospel was advanced through Paul's imprisonment by reason of the favourable effect it had on the other believers in Rome. In Rome a Christian church already existed before Paul's arrival there. To them he had addressed a Letter on an earlier occasion. By his imprisonment the leaders of the church were at first probably filled with a measure of fear and timidity with regard to the public preaching of the gospel in Rome. Now, however, they take courage again, and they become undaunted preachers of the Word of God in the imperial capital. There are, to be sure, still some who are timid and half-hearted; but *"most* of the brethren" take new confidence in the Lord[5] for their task, and that because of Paul's bonds, in which they notice the apostle's courageous endurance of imprisonment for the sake of Christ as well as the safe-keeping of the Lord which he experiences even in

---

5 ἐν κυρίῳ can go with "brethren" (cf. Col. 1:2), but it makes better sense if connected with πεποιθότας as the ground for the hope that revived.

such dismal circumstances. This encourages them to shake off fear and preach the word with enthusiasm, boldness and zeal. They are going to risk it in the hostile city, and they are going to risk more abundantly[6] and speak[7] more fearlessly in public to propagate the teachings of Christ.

The power, emanating from the witness of Paul in his imprisonment, places new confidence in the hearts of his fellow believers, and also lays the Word of God afresh on their lips. All this means progress and advancement of the gospel. Among the praetorian guard *ears,* and among the brethren *mouths* are found for the gospel.

---

[6] The expression *much more* or *more abundantly* suggests that they previously also risked speaking God's Word, but at present were much more bold. Under all circumstances it was a risky thing to preach the gospel in a city like Rome, indifferent and hostile to God as it was.

[7] λαλεῖν is used here instead of the more usual λέγειν to express thereby that with the timid brethren the problem was not only that of speaking or witnessing or preaching in the hostile city, but even the question whether they would *make themselves heard at all,* whether they would open their mouths in the interest of the gospel. λέγειν usually has reference to the sense or meaning, while λαλεῖν rather refers to the voice or sound produced or heard, when speaking. Cf. Kittel IV, p. 75.

1:15—18

15 Some indeed preach Christ even of envy and strife; and some also of good will:

16 the one do it of love, knowing that I am set for the defence of the gospel;

17 but the other proclaim Christ of faction, not sincerely, thinking to raise up affliction for me in my bonds.

18 What then? only that in every way, whether in pretence or in truth, Christ is proclaimed; and therein I rejoice, yea, and will rejoice.

15-17 All who preach Christ in Rome, are not, however, urged by sound motives. All preachers do not show respect, brotherly appreciation and love towards the apostle. The motives for their gospel preaching are not the same with all. Two tendencies are noticeable among them, and in verses 15-17 Paul twice portrays the position that among the Christians and ministers of the gospel at Rome there were some[1] who were of an unkind and envious disposition towards him, and others who were friendly and sympathetically disposed towards him. Of the former it is said that they preach[2] Christ from envy and strife (15), from

---

[1] "Some" may, if logically connected with verse 14, refer to a section of "most of the brethren" mentioned there, who now boldly preach the word. A too close connection with it, however, seems unlikely, as the motives of envy and rivalry would seem incompatible with the "confidence in the Lord" which "most of the brethren" had. Paul seems to refer here in general to preachers in Rome.

[2] The preaching of Christ is expressed here by κηρύσσειν and in verse 17 by καταγγέλλειν. There is really no remarkable difference.

partisanship,[3] not sincerely (17), and in pretence (18).

The idea, that Paul here has in mind the Judaizers, (so among others Bengel, Lightfoot, Meyer, Ellicott), must be rejected, for in these verses no *material* contrast is mentioned between their preaching and that of Paul, but only a *personal* one. Thrice the apostle pertinently declares that they preach Christ (15, 17, 18). The content of their preaching therefore is sound, it contains no heresy or perversion of the gospel, and in that the apostle rejoices (18). Paul's attitude, however, is quite different towards the Judaizers, who, by accentuating the law, preach "another Jesus" or "another gospel" (2 Cor. 11:4, 13), and who are mercilessly castigated and exposed by Paul, especially in his Letter to the Galatians (1:6, 7; 5:1—6), but also later on in this Letter (3:2, 3).

The point in question here is that of a personal antithesis or antipathy, an attitude which was pro-Christ but anti-Paul. It is possible that to a great measure it was a "question of prestige that brought a section of the Christians at Rome in opposition to Paul" (Barth), a prejudice against Paul which sought to take advantage of his captivity, a pettiness

---

The former is usually used in connection with the gospel, with the meaning of: to announce with authority, to act as herald; to the latter the general idea of to proclaim or announce, is attached.

[3] It is to be observed that with the best textual witnesses (Aleph, A B D E F G and others), verses 16 and 17, as found in the T.R. followed by the A.V., appear in reverse order, viz. first verse 17 and after that verse 16. The sequence of the Received Text—supported by K and L—originates from the desire to mention the two sections named in verse 15 in the same order in the verses following, and not to have a chiastic reference, as the authentic text has it. For the real purport of the pericope it makes no difference which sequence is followed.

which revealed itself in the carnal disposition of envy and jealousy over against a more favoured minister of the gospel.

Envy and rivalry and partisanship—born of self-seeking—are the cause why Christ is "not sincerely" proclaimed (literally: not in a holy, pure way). There is an evil motive attached to their preaching; they intend to afflict Paul in his bonds (imprisonment), to aggravate his burden and thereby cause him additional pain and grief, to raise up[4] still more suffering and affliction against him who is already a prisoner.

In favourable contrast with the painful personal antagonism coming from *some* preachers, there is the other section who are sympathetically minded towards Paul, and who preach[5] Christ from good will (15), out of love (16) and in truth (18). Here the motives are pure, and such preaching offers powerful support and encouragement to the apostle and to the cause he advocates, viz. Christ and His gospel. Their love is directed towards the apostle and is motivated by the fact that they know that he is set or destined[6] for the defense of the gospel. For the sake of the gospel as well as for Paul's sake, who is God's instrument for the defense thereof, they lovingly co-operate on behalf of the cause by their

---

4   The reading ἐγείρειν (rouse) has much stronger Mss. support than ἐπιφέρειν (bring to, add to), which probably originated from an attempt to facilitate the original expression.

5   ἐξ ἀγάπης (16) as well as ἐξ ἐριθείας (17) must go with the verb καταγγέλλουσιν, and thus provide a strong repetition of the idea expressed in verse 15.

6   κεῖμαι is to be taken here as meaning "I am put," "I am destined," instead of the literal "I lie" or "I am placed."

preaching. There are no unworthy ulterior motives. They proclaim Christ in truth and sincerity.

18 *What then?*[7] If this is so, that some do not preach Christ from sincere motives and wish to add affliction to Paul in his bonds, what does it matter? What is attained? *Only that*[8] in any case Christ is preached, and that one great favourable result therefore is produced for the cause for which Paul is a prisoner. "In every way" denotes the various ways and motives accompanying the preaching of Christ, and in a last antithesis they are summarised: Christ is proclaimed in pretence or in truth. The preaching under pretence or semblance was a preaching of Christ well enough, but it served as a means of seeking self-glory and of attaining selfish ends. The motive was not sincere, for in reality it concerned rather the person himself than Christ. Over against this there was a preaching without any unworthy personal motives, which was only concerned about the truth, the great cause itself, i.e. it had as its sole object Christ and His glory and the spreading of His gospel.

Anyway, in every case, Christ is proclaimed. Even by insincere preaching, even by jealous and self-seeking preachers, even from wrong underlying motives. The main thing is that Christ is being proclaimed and made known in every way. And in that the apostle rejoices. In all his

---

[7] τί γάρ is to be regarded as a separate exclamation and question, and is rightly followed by a mark of interrogation. A similar instance is found in Rom. 3:3. The question is suggested by the immediately preceding statement.

[8] πλὴν ὅτι is the reading of Aleph, A F G P; πλὴν that of D E K L, while B has ὅτι. The uncommon construction πλὴν ὅτι also appears in Paul's address, reported in Acts 20:23. The use of πλὴν alone is more common (3:16; 4:14).

affliction and personal grief, in all his disapproval of sinful partisanship and insincerity of action and the preaching under a cloak in the case of some preachers, the joy in the progress of the gospel, in the fact that Christ is preached, ever dominates. Not the way he is personally affected by it, but how it affects the cause of Christ is his only care. For Christ, his Lord, and the preaching of His gospel, was the one great passion of his life.[9]

---

[9] The words "and will rejoice" belong, according to the logical context, indicated by the conjunction "for," to verse 19 (so RSV), and not to verse 18, although they make good sense there also. The thoughts of the apostle wander from his present joy (verse 18), concerning the preaching of Christ in all manner or means, to his future joy in respect to his own salvation and the honouring of Christ in all circumstances (19, 20).

CHRIST WILL BE HONOURED, WHETHER BY LIFE
OR BY DEATH

1:19—20

19 For I know that this shall turn out to my salvation, through your supplication and the supply of the Spirit of Jesus Christ,

20 according to my earnest expectation and hope, that in nothing shall I be put to shame, but that with all boldness, as always, so now also Christ shall be magnified in my body, whether by life, or by death.

19 The apostle is quite sure that his present circumstances will turn out for (literally: end in) his deliverance. By this he does not necessarily mean an expected release from prison, for he is taking into account, as appears from verse 20, the possibility of his death. Paul only gives expression to the conviction[1] that everything must work for good with him, for his salvation. Herein his release from prison may be included, but not necessarily. Two factors will be instrumental in order that his unfavourable circumstances may turn out for his good and deliverance. The first of these is the prayer of the church, which he mentions together with the Holy Spirit. "The prayer of the Philippians is not too unimportant, not too human, not too impotent to stand next to that first Magnitude (the Holy Spirit), next to whom, strictly speaking, no second can stand" (Barth). Paul relies on the intercession of the church, for he knows the power of the prayer of faith (cf. Acts 4:29—31; 12:5—12).

---

1 $o\tilde{\imath}\delta a$ here indicates (in contrast with $\gamma\iota\gamma\nu\acute{\omega}\sigma\varkappa\omega$) assured knowledge.

Next to prayer the apostle mentions "the supply[2] of the Spirit[3] of Jesus Christ". The Spirit that dwells in Christ as the head, is also at the disposal of the members of His body on earth. The Spirit will support, will render assistance, for He is given to the believers to lead them (John 15:26) and to help them (Rom. 8:26).

20 The eager expectation[4] and hope which live in the mind of the apostle, concern the apostle himself, in so far as he looks forward to it that he will not be put to shame in anything, will not be ashamed in the end through the fact that he failed as witness of Christ or did not reach his goal or was unworthy of his Master in some way or other. But his expectation and hope are also alive in respect to Christ and the glory of His Name: that He will be magnified, be honoured with all boldness (RSV: full courage),[5] by his public witness and preaching, even as Paul formerly under all circumstances, favourable and unfavourable, preached Christ without fear. Christ will be magnified "in my body" i.e. in the earthly and bodily existence of the apostle, be it in life or in death. The continuation of life in the body would mean a life of continued labour for Christ; the laying down of the body in death would be a sacrificial offering brought to Christ and His cause. Whether he experiences acquittal and new opportunities

---

2 ἐπιχορηγία really means a grant or provision, in the sense of the rendering of what is necessary for assistance or help.

3 The help comes from the Spirit (subj. gen.), is given by the Spirit.

4 For the expression ἀποκαραδοκία, cf. also Rom. 8:19. The literal meaning is: looking forward to something with head erect, yearningly. Therefore: eager longing or expectation.

5 παρρησία usually denotes courage to speak, but here the expression may also mean: openly, publicly. Cf. Col. 2:15.

for service or conviction and death, in both cases Christ would be glorified. The reason for his joy is focussed on this one point: Christ will be honoured. Paul, the slave, will remain small and insignificant, but Christ, his Lord, will be magnified.

TO LIVE OR TO DIE: WHICH SHALL HE CHOOSE?

21 For to me to live is Christ, and to die is gain.

22 But if to live in the flesh,—if this shall bring fruit from my work, then what I shall choose I know not.

23 But I am in a strait betwixt the two, having the desire to depart and be with Christ; for it is very far better:

24 yet to abide in the flesh is more needful for your sake.

21 The possibility of life or death was suggested in verse 20. Now the apostle counterbalances the significance which his life on the one hand and his death on the other hand would have for himself and the church. And, however rich in content life may be for him, it does not necessarily mean that he should wish for a longer life. Death also offered its advantage and its gain.

Paul tersely states his conviction concerning life and death in the well-known words of his: "To me to live[1] is Christ, and to die is gain." Christ is the One and All to give meaning and significance to his existence, the only One who really matters. Christ is all to him—life itself. The apostle is one with Christ and His cause. To know Christ, to love and serve Him, to further His cause, to suffer for Him— that is life to him. "What I live is wholly destined to glorify Christ—the end and purpose of my whole life is Christ and His glory" (Zanchius). Christ lays claim to his whole life.

---

[1] Literally translated: To live for me (is) Christ and to die (is) gain. The expressions τὸ ζῆν and τὸ ἀποθανεῖν instead of the nouns ζωή and θάνατος accentuate the act or process in which life or death exist.

Christ not only lives for him and in him, but has become his very life (cf. 2 Cor. 4:10; 5:15; Col. 3:4; Gal. 2:20).

To die is gain.[2] In a twofold sense death would be gain to him, above all with which he had been favoured in this earthly life. For himself it would mean the glory of heaven, a "being with Christ" (verse 23), a being at home with the Lord (2 Cor. 5:8), the crown of righteousness after the fight (2 Tim. 4:7, 8), in short: the indescribable heavenly bliss. But the gain would not only be directed towards him as an apostle ; Christ also would be better honoured (verse 20), as in death all is done away with that still resisted the full development of the life of Christ in him, and all infirmity and sin which still stood in the way of magnifying Christ. After death there would be a fuller and greater glorification of the Lord.

22 To die is gain; would the apostle then prefer it? Or was there still some sense in a continued earthly life?[3] Yes,

---

[2] Interesting, but, seen from a grammatical and linguistic point of view not very successful, is the view held by Calvin, which makes Christ the subject of both clauses and then translates thus: "For Christ is to me in life and in death gain" (Mihi enim vivendo Christus est et moriendo lucrum). Such an interpretation, however, does not suit well the Greek construction and context. The most natural rendering of the sentence takes the words in the order in which they stand: For to live is Christ to me, and to die gain. The verb *is* is understood.

[3] Calvin (later also Lightfoot) regards εἰ as interrogative: "What if my life in the flesh is the fruit of labour (will bring fruit with it) ?"

Many exegetes take both the first sections as introductory clause or protasis, governed by εἰ, and then translate: "But if life in the flesh, (if) it means fruitful labour for me, then: which I shall choose, I cannot tell." (So amongst others Vincent, Meyer, Ellicott, Eadie). It, however, takes no account of the fact that with Paul there was no uncertainty about the question whether longer labour would mean fruitful labour, life⁴ in the flesh,⁵ a prolongation of the earthly, bodily life, would have fruitful labour⁶ as a result, more opportunity for labour and more fruit of labour, more service to the cause of Christ on earth. The apostle does not know and cannot tell⁷ what he would like to choose—death which is gain or life which can offer the fruit of labour to his Master. It remains a difficult decision.

23-24 Once again Paul weighs the implications of death and life as against each other. He is hard pressed between the two (literally: kept together by the two). There is so much to be said for both sides. He has a desire to depart, i.e. to be loosened⁸ from this earthly life and to be with Christ. Then he would see what now he believed, and

for it was "more needful for your sake" (24). εἰ can therefore not govern that clause.

⁴ We have an elliptical sentence here (as in the verse preceding) in which the verb is understood. ἐστίν μοι lends itself to this purpose, and we could therefore translate: "If, however, to live in the flesh *is for me* (i.e. is destined for me, is granted to me, is my share), then *it is* (means) fruitful labour for me." See also Kennedy, ad hoc.

⁵ σάρξ here is not meant in a sinful ethical sense, as for instance in Rom 8:5, but is used instead of σῶμα to express the weak, transitory nature of the physical body.

⁶ Literally: fruit of labour, i.e. the fruit that follows on labour, the fruit produced or attained by labour.

⁷ γνωρίζειν sometimes means: to know. In most cases in the N. T., however, it has the meaning of: to explain, declare, say, tell. It is therefore very probable that Paul uses the word here in the latter sense: "What I shall choose I do not say, I cannot tell, I cannot declare."

⁸ ἀναλύειν means: to loosen. The figure here is that of a ship loosened from its anchorage, in order to continue its course; or also of a tent which is unfastened and struck down, to be pitched again elsewhere. To be loosened therefore means: to go forth, to depart.

the utmost bliss would be enjoyed when he would be with Christ—not only in His presence but also forever united with Him in glory. This would be an immediate union with Christ, directly after death. No mention here of an intermediate state of unconsciousness or sleep of the soul in which Christ's presence would not be experienced; and also no thought that he would be with Christ only after the resurrection. Such an immediate being-with-Christ is far better[9] than the continuance of the earthly life.

And yet—"to abide in the flesh is more needful for your sake." Over against his personally directed desire for the very best, he now weighs the interests of the church, the necessity of staying in life still longer for their sake. Not the gain, not his own heart's desire, but the need of the church and his God-given calling in their behalf becomes the urge that ultimately determines his expectation for the future (25). The church still needs him, the young church emerging from heathendom cannot yet do without his guidance, advice and help. For their sake it was necessary for Paul to live still longer. To be with Christ was better, to remain with them more necessary.

---

9   A double comparative in the original. Literally we have: "For it is much more the better," i.e. much, much better; by far better.

CONVICTION THAT HE WILL LIVE TO
VISIT THEM AGAIN

1:25, 26

> 25 And having this confidence, I know that I shall abide,
> yea, and abide with you all, for your progress and joy in
> the faith;
>
> 26 that your glorying may abound in Christ Jesus in me
> through my presence with you again.

25 This verse refers to the whole foregoing portion,[1]
verses 19 to 24. Paul knows that all will turn out for his
own good (19), and that in everything Christ will be
magnified, whether it be by life or by death (20). And with
the conviction that life would mean fruitful labour (23),
and that it was necessary for the church's sake (24), he adds
in full assurance: "And having this confidence, I know that
I shall abide," or, in other words: "that God's way for me
means longer life and continued labour." He would be
with them again, as would be made possible for him through
release from his present captivity. The apostle possibly has
in mind a wider circle of Christian churches, and not only
Philippi, when he states that he will "abide with you all,
for your progress and joy in the faith." His continued life,
necessary for the church, and his remaining with them,[2]

---

[1] The view that the first clause does not allude to anything in the
foregoing portion, that πεποιθώς is to be taken with the verb οἶδα,
and that τοῦτο refers to the statement following, introduced by ὅτι
(thus Lightfoot, Zahn, et al.), so that the sentence runs as follows:
"This I know assuredly that . . .," does not do justice to Paul's preceding
argument.

[2] In the verb παραμενῶ the prefix παρα- emphasises the idea of

would serve their advancement and joy in the faith. In their life of faith growth, development and progress were indispensable; knowledge of Christ and love of Him, obedience to Him and trust in Him had to increase, and the growing faith had to be accompanied by joy as the natural sequence of sure faith. "Progressiveness and joyfulness alike characterise faith" (Vincent).

26 By such sentiment Christ would be magnified. Not Paul, nor the church, would receive praise for it, but ground and reason for praise would be in Christ, because His cause would once more be advanced, and His gospel again be proclaimed among them by the apostle. Because of the apostle as the bearer of the gospel of Christ and the instrument through which Christ magnified Himself in their midst, and through his presence once again[3] with them, Christ would be abundantly praised. He would grant them the privilege of being together, and for that He alone would deserve thanks and praise and glory.

And so the apostle here makes mention of his positive anticipation and hope to be with them once more, and therefore to be released from his imprisonment. Without adequate knowledge of the subsequent course of events, it is impossible to say how far this anticipation was realised. The narrative of the Acts closes with the mention of his imprisonment in Rome. He was either never released from prison, so that this was his last imprisonment, and his expectation of being with the Philippians again was not

---

with: remain with you. In some Mss. the still stronger variant συμπαραμενῶ is found.

[3] The word πάλιν alludes to his former visits to them on different occasions, and his intention of being with them once more, after his expected release.

realised, or—and this is more likely—he was released[4] from this imprisonment, visited several churches and undertook more missionary journeys, was taken prisoner again (a few years after his first imprisonment in Rome), and thereupon died a martyr's death.

---

[4] The probability is indeed very great that Paul was released from this first imprisonment in Rome, and that he undertook a fourth missionary journey, in which his wish to visit Spain, was fulfilled.

From the Pastoral Letters it would appear that Paul undertook travels and had experiences of which Acts makes no mention, and which probably took place after his (first) imprisonment. He was in Crete a short while ago (Tit. 1:5), decided to spend the winter in Nicopolis (Tit. 3:12), was in Macedonia shortly before (1 Tim. 1:3); and when in prison again, he mentions the fact that he was in Troas a short time before (2 Tim. 4:13), and in Miletus where he left Trophimus ill (2 Tim. 4:20); and he makes definite mention of a former trial and release: "At my first defence no one took my part... But the Lord stood by me and gave me strength to proclaim the word fully, that all the Gentiles might hear it. So I was rescued from the lion's mouth" (2 Tim. 4:16, 17).

The testimony of several ancient Christian writers supports the view that Paul was released and that he went to the "extreme West" (Is this Spain, as seen from Rome?). Clemens Romanus (end of the first century), the Muratorian Fragment (c. 170 A.D.), the fathers Eusebius (obiit 338), Chrysostomus (obiit 407), and Hieronymus (obiit 420), can be quoted in support. The words of Eusebius are representative of their opinion: "Having defended himself successfully, it is generally asserted that Paul went out again to preach the gospel, and later on went to Rome for the second time and there died a martyr's death under Nero" (Hist. Eccl. II, 22, 2).

ADMONITION TO STEADFASTNESS IN ALL
CIRCUMSTANCES

1:27—30

27 Only let your manner of life be worthy of the gospel of
Christ: that, whether I come and see you or be absent,
I may hear of your state, that ye stand fast in one spirit,
with one soul, striving for the faith of the gospel;

28 and in nothing affrighted by the adversaries: which is for
them an evident token of perdition, but of your salvation,
and that from God;

29 because to you it hath been granted in the behalf of
Christ, not only to believe on him, but also to suffer in
his behalf:

30 having the same conflict which ye saw in me, and now
hear to be in me.

27 After expressing his confidence that he would be
with them again, the apostle nevertheless once more refers
to the twofold possibility that he may come and see them,
or may be absent and only be informed of their circumstances. The main thing, however, is not whether he will
be able to come or not, but whether Christ will be magnified in the church's manner of life. Only—and this is the
one thing that matters—whatever may happen to the
apostle, the members of the church, as citizens of the
heavenly kingdom, should live[1] worthy of the gospel of

---

[1] πολιτεύεσθε refers in the first instance to the behaviour or conduct
of a citizen of the state, and means: exercise your citizenship, or:
act (live) as a citizen. In the use of this word an allusion to the
heavenly citizenship of believers can be traced, to their conduct or
manner of life as subjects of the Kingdom of God, as distinctly stated
elsewhere, cf. 3:20. The word otherwise generally used by Paul is

Christat,[2] i.e. in agreement with the obligations which the gospel imposes, the privileges which it brings along, and the high calling with which it comes to man. For the apostle—whether he himself is present or absent—longs to hear[3] that concerning them which will reveal a conduct worthy of the gospel, viz. that they stand firm and inwardly bound together in the common fight of faith. Steadfastness and unanimity (cf. also 2:2), are necessary requirements for all believers. The same mind and one spirit[4] of unshakeable steadfastness must be theirs (for they have to cope with opponents (28), suffering (29) and conflict (30), and with one mind they must strive side by side in the struggle of faith. In spirit and soul,[5] in mind and feeling, in thought and desire, the believers must be bound together in a unity[6]

πεϱιπατεῖν (to walk, to live, without any further association with the state or the Kingdom of God), cf. 3:17, 18; Rom. 6:4; Eph. 4:1.

[2] The genitive τοῦ χϱιστοῦ can be taken both as subj. gen. and as obj. gen. The gospel emanating from Christ is also the gospel concerning Christ. Christ is both author and content of the gospel.

[3] In the extant Mss. the present tense ἀϰούω alternates with the future ἀϰούσω. The meaning remains essentially the same. The former reading, however, is better accredited.

[4] ἐν ἑνὶ πνεύματι can allude to the Holy Spirit (the One Spirit in all the members of the body of Christ), but must rather be understood here in a general sense as unity of spirit and insight, worked in man by the Holy Ghost.

[5] The contrast between ψυχή and πνεῦμα (where they do not appear as synonyms, as is often the case) lies in the fact that ψυχή denotes more especially the inward feeling and will, the soul as the seat of desires and emotions, whereas with πνεῦμα the emphasis falls on the mind or spirit with its activities of thought and reflection.

[6] Karl Barth observes that unity of spirit is not a task but a gift, of which man should just remind himself so as to be of one mind; but unity of soul is a task, and man must be delivered from his soul's

which encompasses their inward disposition as well as their outward action, and makes them strive[7] shoulder to shoulder as comrades instilled with the same motive to pursue to the end the fight for victory. For in this fight "the faith[8] of the gospel" is at stake, the contents of the faith as well as the possession of the faith which the gospel offers, and which is centred in Christ. "Not the subjective conditions of faith is the point at issue here, but the one faith, which according to its nature and contents is defined in Scripture as the only means of salvation" (Greijdanus). The Christian's fight is not described here as against anybody or anything, but as *for* the faith, for the gospel truth.

28 The firm stand of the church will also become manifest in so far as the believers are not frightened,[9] terrified or intimidated by the action of the adversaries. It is not definitely stated who those opponent are, but probably Paul does not refer to false teachers or seducers, but to aggressive and hostile Jews or Gentiles, who would use affliction and persecution to withstand the gospel and to terrorise and intimidate its followers. "That the Christians must not

---

antipathies before he can really with one mind take a firm stand against common difficulties (Comm. *ad loc.*).

[7] The image suggested by the verb here, is that of a race or contest where participants compete for the prize or crown.

[8] The expression $τ\tilde{η}$ $πίστει$ $το\tilde{υ}$ $εὐαγγελίου$, in this particular combination, appears only here in the N. T. It can be translated: *by* (or *through*) the faith of the gospel; but a more natural rendering would be: *for* the faith of the gospel, whereby the purpose of the common struggle is emphasised. $πίστις$ is to be taken here in its objective meaning, viz. as the contents of faith. Cf. Jude 3.

[9] Literally: "not frightened in nothing by the opponents." $πτυρόμενοι$ really means: becoming shy or skittish or scared—a figure used of frightened horses.

allow themselves in the least to be terrified, impressed or bluffed by the opponents, that they must not even make the least concession to them, but that they must entirely follow their own principles which they have chosen for themselves—this is what Paul means by *stand firm*" (Barth).

The steadfastness and undauntedness of the believers is at the same time a token[10] of perdition to those who thwart the gospel, a sure sign of the futility of their attempts to oppose God and His cause, whereby only their own destruction is effected. He who despises and opposes the grace of Christ is lost. On the other hand, the steadfastness of the believers during strife and affliction is an indication and sure sign of their own deliverance and salvation, for only saints, the truly saved, are capable of such perseverance. A persevering faith comes from God and is the fruit of His grace. It bears witness to the fact that it is God Himself Who graciously strengthens and keeps. After all, it is God who completes the good work which He began in them (verse 6).

29-30 Opposition and antagonism bring along suffering—suffering granted or "graciously given" by God, because it is "in behalf of Christ." (Cf. 1 Pet. 4:13, 14). Twice the expression "in behalf of Christ" is used in the sentence. Faith in Christ and suffering for Christ, both are there for the sake of Christ and for His glorification, and both are graciously given to man. First of all faith, which does not exist merely in accepting the truths concerning Christ intellectually, but is the soul's going out to Christ in personal trust and hearty surrender. Such a faith is a

---

10   The feminine form ἥτις (instead of ὅ τι) is used here to go with ἔνδειξις. Literally we have: "which is a clear omen, etc.," referring to the whole preceding idea of steadfastness and undauntedness.

gift of grace, wrought in the heart by God's Spirit and granted by divine favour (Eph. 2:8).

On account of his connection with Christ, suffering, however, is also inflicted upon the believer, with the purpose of doing harm to the cause of Christ. An ordeal of affliction and persecution has to be endured "for the sake of Christ", but thereby at the same time the faith is proved as genuine. The true faith leads to fellowship with the suffering of Christ, and the grace of God reveals itself in the fact that man is able to suffer and be brought as an offering for the cause of Christ (cf. 2:17; Col. 1:24).

The fight of faith is common to all believers. In verse 27 the idea of comrades in the fight was already alluded to, and here that connection between the apostle and the church is emphasised anew. In its nature and essence it is the same conflict[11] with all, the same exertion and struggle, self-denial and hardship, which the fighter has to endure if he is to conquer. The church *saw* this in Paul when at Philippi he had to do with opposition and had to endure flogging and imprisonment (Acts 16:19ff.); and now they *hear* it from him, because also in Rome he was experiencing personal conflict, affliction and captivity, as both the Letter (from verse 12) and Epaphroditus (2:25) could inform them. For the apostle as for the Church, there was the same fight and the same suffering in the behalf of Christ.

---

11   ἀγών refers to a contest in the athletic games, with all the strife, exertion, struggle and hardship connected therewith. Cf. 2 Tim. 4:7, 8. Also Kittel, *TWNT*, I, p. 136 ff.

CHAPTER II

EXHORTATION TO UNANIMITY AND HUMILITY

2:1—4

1 If there is therefore any exhortation in Christ, if any consolation of love, if any fellowship of the Spirit, if any tender mercies and compassions,

2 make full my joy, that ye be of the same mind, having the same love, being of one accord, of one mind;

3 doing nothing through faction or through vainglory, but in lowliness of mind each counting other better than himself;

4 not looking each of you to his own things, but each of you also to the things of others.

1 By a fourfold repetition of *if* and *any*,[1] and the accumulation of Christian experiences which are self-evident to the readers, the argument is not only stated forcefully, but the exhortation following in verse 2 (and related to the main idea of the foregoing pericope and especially verse 27, viz. steadfast unanimity) is introduced by a fourfold motive.

(1) If there is any admonition, encouragement, or exhortation[2] *in Christ:* i.e. derived from our fellowship with Christ, which we have to exercise for the sake of Christ.

---

[1] With each subordinate clause introduced by εἰ, the accompanying verb ἐστιν is understood. The manner of expression is compact and forcible.

[2] παράκλησις can be translated by "comfort" or "consolation" (Luke 2:25; 2 Cor. 1:3, 4; 7:4), but also by "exhortation" (Acts 13:15, Rom. 12:8; cf. Heb. 13:22). The latter is not only the most usual with Paul, but also fits well here.

72

(2) If there is any stimulus or incentive[3] of love: "if love has any persuasive power to move you to concord" (Vincent). (3) If there is any fellowship of the Spirit: any participation in the Spirit, any fellowship with the Holy Ghost and mutual fellowship in the Spirit. (4) If there is any affection[4] and sympathy,[5] tender and sensitive mercy. If these spiritual experiences with which the Philippians are acquainted are present, they have to serve as the basis for the deeper oneness in heart and soul to which the apostle exhorts them.

2 It will promote the advancement and completion[6]

---

[3] Rightly: incentive (RSV), encouragement, not *consolation* (ASV). In 1 Thess. 5:14 we find both ideas of exhortation and encouragement next to each other.

[4] Literally σπλάγχνα means the inward parts, as seat of the emotional life. τις σπλάγχνα is the version of most of the oldest Mss. (Aleph, A, B, C, D), over against τίνα in a few later minuscules. The form is irregular and difficult to explain. Is it a solecism of the apostle, or is it used here in an undeclined form for the sake of the symmetry of the four clauses following one another?

[5] Many Greek fathers, and later on also Calvin, interpret this verse as referring to the relation of the Philippians to Paul personally in the sense of: "If there is any affection and encouragement etc. in you *for me*, if you have sympathy *with me* in my suffering, etc., then complete my joy." This rendering is, however, unlikely. For it would then seem as if it was the prisoner Paul who needed exhortation and encouragement, whereas he expressly makes mention of his joy, which must be made full (verse 2). We must keep in mind—as Greijdanus rightly comments *ad hoc*—that the apostle wishes to stir the Philippians to action, and bring them to be of the same mind and to have the same love, etc. (verse 2)—and with that in view he names various motives in verse 1. It is the apostle who addresses and encourages the church, not *vice versa*.

[6] πληρώσατε presupposes that Paul already knows joy, cf. 1:4, but that his cup can be made full or fuller.

of the apostle's joy, if the church is unanimous,[7] of the same mind (literally: contemplating the same thing). This will reveal itself first of all in that they have the same love, viz. towards God and Jesus Christ, and in Him mutually towards each other, and in addition to this that they are "of one accord, of one mind" (literally: together in soul contemplating the one thing),[8] driven by the same urge and desire, and directing their thoughts and endeavour on that one thing,[9] viz. the cause of Christ and its furtherance through unamity and concord amongst the believers.

3 The trend of thought (one in love, one in soul, one in mind) pointed towards the binding power of the Christian faith. But in addition to that a warning is added against dispositions which ought *not* to be found in the

---

[7] ἵνα must not be translated here by *in order that*. It is not the purpose of the joy that is accentuated, but the ground or means for its accomplishment. Translation: because you consider the same (thing), or are of the same mind; "by being of the same mind" (RSV).

[8] It undoubtedly is best not to take συνψύχοι separately, disconnecting it from the following clause with a comma, but, in the light of the construction of the whole sentence with the four consecutive participles, rather to take συνψύχοι with τὸ ἓν φρονοῦντες, by which literally is meant: "Together in soul considering the one thing" (thus Meyer, Vincent, Alford and others). That in such a case the adverb συνψύχως would have been more in place than the adjectival form συνψύχοι, need not be a serious difficulty.

[9] Some Mss. (e.g. A and C) in the second instance also have τὸ αὐτό instead of τὸ ἓν, which can be explained by the tendency to make the second expression correspond exactly with the first. In τὸ αὐτὸ φρονεῖν the unanimity is stated in general; by τὸ ἓν φρονεῖν the object of the unanimity is more concretely indicated, which for that matter is the same in both cases, although it is not further described.

church of Christ. Nothing must be done or contemplated[10] from selfishness or conceit. There must be no self-seeking, no sinful egotism; and also no conceit or pride which is vain and without content on account of self-imagined excellence. For such a disposition which seeks and prides itself is carnal and unworthy of a Christian. At Philippi they were acquainted with Judaizers who prided themselves on their observance of the law and circumcision, as well as with Greeks who found occasion for vainglorious self-exaltation in the wisdom of this world and the heights of their cultural attainments. Such, however, was not the Christian way.

Such a mind, furthermore, is adverse to the spirit of unity in the church, for it seeks itself and breaks up the fellowship. Instead of this each should in humility count the other better than himself. Humility, a modest opinion of oneself, meekness, and an insight in one's own insignificance, is the opposite of self-exaltation, and it counts the other, i.e. the fellow-man better and more excellent than himself.[11] Such a disposition will promote unity, for it binds believers together in mutual interest, respect and appreciation.

4 Everyone must not look to his own interests only, but also[12] to that of others. Unselfishness and consideration

---

10 Instead of a presupposed ποιοῦντες, a presupposed φρονοῦντες will better fit in with the trend of the preceding clause: "Contemplate nothing" instead of "Do nothing . . ."

11 That believers can reasonably regard others or each other (ἀλλήλους) in such a way, finds its ground (as Greijdanus rightly observes) in the variety of talents which are granted to believers, so that the one can always appreciate something in the other in which he excells.

12 The expression *but . . . also* assumes that one may rightfully see

towards others is the right and God-pleasing disposition. Selfishness which thinks only of its own interests and seeks itself, fails to appreciate the fellow-man and is blind to his interests. On the other hand humility and love direct our thoughts and consideration towards the advancement of the interests of others. For man is never alone, there is always still the "other one"; and things never concern himself only, but also the other one, for whose good and welfare he should care, and whose interests he should promote in utter self-forgetfulness. For the Christian there is no road that by-passes his fellowman.

---

to one's own interests, but that in addition to that the interests of others should also be minded. You must love your neighbour as yourself.

2:5—8

> 5 Have this mind in you, which was also in Christ Jesus:
> 6 who, existing in the form of God, counted not the being on an equality with God a thing to be grasped,
> 7 but emptied himself, taking the form of a servant, being made in the likeness of men;
> 8 and being found in fashion as a man, he humbled himself, becoming obedient even unto death, yea, the death of the cross.

5 The highest example of such a self-forgetful regard for the interests of others is now portrayed, viz. the condescension of Christ in His incarnation. In Him believers have the perfect example of how they should behave, an example of humility and self-renunciation with a view to the welfare of others. A high demand is made here upon the inward disposition of believers: "Have this mind in you (literally: contemplate[1] this in yourselves) which was also in Christ Jesus."

In the midst of the practical and paranetic portion of the Letter with its exhortation to meekness and to a way of life which does not seek its own interests, a few verses now follow which are not without difficulties for the interpreter of Scripture, and which treat of the mystery of the incarnation of Christ, His self-emptying, His humiliation and eventual exaltation,—a profound Christological argument

---

[1] The reading φρονεῖτε is better supported and to be preferred to the passive φρονείσθω. The insertion of γὰρ as connecting word with the previous verses, is not supported by the oldest manuscripts, not being found in Aleph A B C.

in which the understanding of each word and phrase is of great importance, and which can indeed be described as a "Christ-hymn" without parallel.

6 First of all it is said of Christ, the *Logos asarkos*, the Word not yet made flesh, that He was "in the form of God." The verb here used[2] by the apostle denotes that both the previous existence of Christ and His continued existence afterwards was "in the form of God." By the "form of God" is meant neither the abstract essence or being of God, nor merely an external form or appearance of God,[3] but His divine nature, which is inseparable from His person and

---

[2] ὑπάρχων is used here instead of the much more usual ὤν. It suggests a much fuller meaning, and as an imperfect participle it denotes continued action. "Contrasted with the following aorists it points to indefinite continuance of being" (Gwynn, *Speakers Comm.* ad hoc). "It expresses continuance of an antecedent state or condition" (Gifford, *The Incarnation,* pp. 14 ff). In both other instances where Paul connects ὑπάρχων with the aorist (2 Cor. 8:17, Rom. 4:19), it denotes continuance.

[3] μορφή cannot be considered identical with οὐσία (as Augustine has it), because it does not denote the abstract being but the concrete nature and attributes, nor can it be put on a level with the outward, changeable form or appearance. The difference between μορφή and σχῆμα should be noted. From the N. T. use of the words it would appear that the idea of changeableness and instability is attached to σχῆμα (1 Cor. 7:31, 2 Cor. 11:13—15), and that on the other hand μορφή (in instances such as Rom. 8:29, Phil. 3:10, 2 Cor. 3:18, Gal. 4:19) denotes the inner being as it actually and concretely realises itself in the individual. "It remains that μορφή θεοῦ must apply to the attributes of the Godhead" (Lightfoot, Comm., pp. 130—138, in a note on the use of the above-mentioned words). See also Vincent, Comm. *ad loc.*: "μορφή here means that expression of being which is identified with the essential nature and character of God and which reveals it."

in which the Divine Being realises Himself in His immanent, inherent, divine glory and godly attributes.

The pre-existent Christ who was in the form of God "counted not the being on an equality with God[4] (better translated: "existence in a manner equal to God") a thing to be grasped." "A thing to be grasped" is perhaps not the best rendering for the original word, which means "robbery." And according to this connotation of the word, an "existence in a manner equal to God" was not "a thing to be robbed or grasped," for it was not something which the Logos, Christ, still had to acquire, but which was His already. It was a dignity which belonged to the pre-existent Christ, to which He was entitled, and a right which He actually possessed. The original word must therefore be taken in the passive sense[5] of "something robbed or grasped," a costly

---

[4] τὸ εἶναι ἴσα θεῷ must be translated: "to be in such a manner as God" or "to exist in a manner equal to God, or in a manner like unto God," and not: "to be equal to God." The expression is not identical with ἐν μορφῇ θεοῦ ὑπάρχων, although it is very closely related to it. ἴσα is used adverbially and means: in such a way or manner. It does not, therefore, denote equality of being, which is already expressed by μορφή θεοῦ, and in which case ἴσον would have been substituted for ἴσα. Where this difference is not noted, the two expressions ἐν μορφῇ θεοῦ ὑπάρχων and τὸ εἶναι ἴσα θεῷ are wrongly considered identical in meaning. For this reason the Vulgate rendering esse se aequalem Deo cannot be deemed correct.

[5] ἁρπαγμός does not here denote actio rapiendi or res rapienda but res rapta. Although ἅρπαγμα would probably suit this connotation better, we find in Scripture more endings in -μος used in a passive meaning. Cf. Eadie, Comm. ad hoc., p. 103. In combination with ἡγεῖσθαι the expression ἁρπαγμός is used to denote a much valued possession or gain, and the pregnant meaning of "robbery" has been ousted.

possession, a highly esteemed prize or gain. In such a light Christ did not regard His existence-in-a-manner-equal-to-God: it was not as something precious which was robbed, "a prize which must not slip from His grasp, a treasure to be clutched and retained at all hazards" (Lightfoot). Christ could have existed and have appeared only as God, only in a manner equal to God: it was a right which was due to Him; He need not have gone into another manner of existence. But as such a valuable possession, or a thing grasped which desperately had to be clung to at all costs, He did not regard it. In His adorable love and grace He was willing through His incarnation to enter into another—a more humble—manner of existence and to take the form of a servant.

The expression "equality with God" (which is not a very literal or accurate rendering of the original) does not therefore here denote His essential equality with God nor His identity of being with God, but describes His manner of existence as God, by which is meant His divine "existential glory, the majesty of His revelation, the greatness and splendour of His manner of being" (Greijdanus).

7 Christ was in the form of God and existed in a manner equal to God, but He emptied Himself.[6] In a literal and absolute sense He could not have emptied Himself of His divine essence or nature, for by so doing He would have ceased to be God. Therefore a metaphorical sense is to be attached to the verb "empty," as is the case in the four other

---

6 κενοῦν (κενόω) means (according to Cremer, *Bibl.-theol. Wörterbuch*, p. 352): (a) to empty in an absolute sense; (b) to empty in a relative sense, with the genitive (of contents) following the verb, and c) to empty in a metaphorical sense, i.e. to bring to nought, to make worthless, without effect. Cf. also Kittel III, p. 661.

instances where Paul uses this word. He asserts, for instance, that the faith, the cross, or his boasting can be "emptied" (cf. Rom. 4:14, 1 Cor. 1:17, 9:15, 2 Cor. 9:3), and there the word has the meaning of "to make null and void," "to make of no effect," "to empty of its power." (In the A.V. the rendering of our verse is: "He made Himself of no reputation," while the Dutch Statenvertaling translated it by: "Hij heeft Zichzelven vernietigd").

To the question: Of what did Christ empty Himself? this verse gives no answer. Many expositors take it to mean that He emptied Himself of the "form of God" or of the "existence in a manner equal to God," but the verse does not justify such an interpretation. It does not state: "But He emptied Himself *of it*," nor is anything else definitely mentioned whereof He actually emptied Himself. If Calvin therefore asserts that He emptied Himself of His majesty and glory (Comm. ad hoc), and Lightfoot says: "He divested Himself . . . of the glories, the prerogatives of deity" (Comm. ad hoc), then this is no legitimate deduction from the phrase in question, but a bold conclusion based on the subsequent statement that He took the form of a servant.

And yet the apostle does not omit to say in which respect and in what way Christ "emptied" Himself, according to his use of the word. The kenosis (emptying) of Christ namely existed in His "taking the form of a servant" and "being made in the likeness of men."[7]

---

[7] "The word ἐκένωσεν was evidently selected as a peculiarly strong expression of the entireness of Jesus' self-renunciation, and in order to throw the pre-incarnate glory and the incarnate humiliation into sharp contrast . . . Its most satisfactory definition is found in the succeeding details which describe the incidents of Christ's humanity, and with these exegesis is compelled to stop" (M. R. Vincent, Excursus on vss. 6—11, in I.C.C.).

He took the form of a servant. This explains the *how* of
the kenosis. Logically and temporally the taking on of the form
of a servant coincides with the emptying. By taking[8] the form
of a servant He emptied Himself. Nothing is mentioned
of any abandonment of divine attributes, the divine nature
or the form of God, but only a divine paradox is stated
here: He emptied Himself by taking something to Himself,
namely the manner of being, the nature or form of a servant
or slave. At His incarnation He remained "in the form of
God" and as such He was Lord and Ruler over all, but He
also accepted the nature of a servant as part of His humanity.
He came to serve. He was not revealing Himself on earth
in glorious or glorified human form, but in the humble
form of a servant. The expression "form of a servant"
denotes more than just the "form of man"; it depicts ser-
vitude and subjection, unattractiveness and lack of distinc-
tion, which were essential characteristics of the humanity
which Christ adopted.

Simultaneously with the taking of the form of a servant
Christ "was made in the likeness of men". This denotes the
human manner of existence into which Christ entered and
which agrees with what in the divine sphere is called the
"existence in a manner equal to God." Christ who existed
in a manner equal to God now also became like unto men.
This coming (being born) in the likeness of men was not
merely the taking of the human form, but the taking of the
form of a servant. It was the fallen, weak human nature
which He accepted. He did not come on earth as king in

---

8   The aorist participle denotes simultaneous action. Therefore the
meaning is: "He emptied Himself *by taking* the form of a servant."
Comp. "by taking" (Vincent, Lightfoot); "dadurch dass er Sklaven-
gestalt nahm" (Meyer, Ewald).

the power and splendour of a glorified human nature, in such a way as that in which He is going to reveal Himself on the day of His parousia, or as that in which He exists now in His state of exaltation, clad with power and majesty also in His human nature. But He came as an ordinary man, in all things made like unto us (sin excepted), in the form of a servant in which the divine glory did not reveal itself.

This acceptance of the form of a servant by the eternal Son of God, and His becoming like unto men by His incarnation, describes the kenosis or emptying of Christ.[9]

---

[9] Apart from exegetical considerations, grave objections of a dogmatic nature can be launched against the modern kenotic theory. Appealing to Phil. 2:7 f., 2 Cor. 8:9, John 17:5, Mark 13:32 and the like, it maintains that the kenosis consisted in a real self-emptying of Christ at His incarnation by a total or partial abandonment of His divine attributes and an abdication of any divine prerogative inconsistent with a proper human experience.

In the main there are three distinct types of kenotic theory, according to which Christ "emptied" Himself:

(a) by laying down some of His divine (the so-called relative) attributes, such as omnipotence, omniscience and omnipresence (Thomasius, Kaftan, Delitzsch, Lange, et al.),

or (b) by parting with and giving up all (metaphysical and ethical) attributes of the Godhead in order to *become* man in the most pregnant sense of the word (Liebner, Gess, Godet, Hofmann, et al.),

or (c) by abandoning the divine mode of existence in order to assume the human (Ebrard, Martensen, Van Oosterzee, Bruce, Gore, Fairbairn, Denney, Mackintosh, et al.).

The main relevant objections to this theory can be summarised as follows:

1. The kenotic theory affects—and annuls—the scriptural doctrine of the Trinity, if one of the adorable Persons of the Holy Trinity, the Son, by giving up His divine attributes or divine manner of existence

ceases for a time to be God, or ceases to be omnipotent, omniscient and omnipresent, while the Father and the Holy Ghost still exercise those attributes which—like all other divine attributes—are essential attributes of deity.

In such a case also the eternal generation of the Son (the forth-streaming of the divine life of the Son out of the Father) would be brought to a stand during the time of the kenosis, as well as the eternal spiration of the Holy Ghost, as the Spirit flows forth out of the Father *and the Son* (Filioque). The second Person of the Godhead cannot be severed from the first and third Persons in such a way, without exchanging the doctrine of the Trinity for tri-theism.

2. The kenotic doctrine affects the received doctrine of the immutability of God. God the Son (according to this theory) is changeable. He could lay down His divine mode of existence and exchange it for a human one; He could part with His divine attributes at His incarnation and take them back at His resurrection. An essential change of some kind or other is hereby introduced in the eternal God, the unchanging "I am that I am." The Scriptures teach and the Church confessed through all the ages that Christ remained what He was (truly God) even when He became what He was not (truly man).

3. The kenotic theory imperils and destroys the true deity of the eternal Son. By parting with some or all of His divine attributes, the Son did not give up something accidental or dispensable but essential and identical with God's being—and such could not happen without thereby extinguishing the divine Being Himself. Christ without divine attributes is not truly God; and a God who has incapacitated Himself to such an extent, in order to become man, that He has abandoned His divine manner of existence, is no real God any longer.

4. The kenotic theory makes the mediatorship of Christ impossible. If Christ lay down His divine attributes or ceased for a time to exist in a manner equal to God, His self-humiliation loses its soteriological significance and His conciliatory work of grace its saving power. For He was not very God and very man then, no true mediator between God and man. Christ without divine attributes is no God-man, but only man.

5. The Christ of the kenotic theory is neither the Christ of the Scriptures nor the Christ of the Creeds of the Church. The Scriptures reveal a Christ who was at the same time truly God and truly man —the mystery of two natures united in one Person—and the Gospels give abundant evidence of the two lines of attributes—the divine and the human—both ascribed to Christ in His earthly life.

The Creeds of the Church tried to formulate this profound Scriptural truth concerning the mystery of the God-man.

In the fifth century the Council of Chalcedon confessed "our Lord Jesus Christ, the same perfect in deity and the same perfect in humanity, truly God and the same truly man ... one and the same Christ, Son, Lord, Only-begotten, manifested in two natures, without confusion, without conversion, indivisibly, inseparably ... the property of each preserved and combined into one person and one hypostasis ..."

The Creeds of the Churches of the Reformation follow the same line. The Lutheran Augsburg Confession mentions "unus Christus, vere Deus et vere homo," and the Formula Concordiae confesses two "distinctae naturae, in sua essentia et proprietatibus naturalibus, inconfusae."

The Reformed Westminster Confession states that in Christ incarnate "two whole, perfect and distinct natures, the Godhead and the manhood, were inseparably joined together in one person ... very God and very man, yet one Christ ..."

The Confessio Belgica or Nederlandsche Geloofsbelijdenis (creed of the Dutch Calvinistic Churches) speaks very distinctly of "twee natuuren in één eenigen persoon vereenigd, doch elke natuur hare onderscheiden eigenschappen behoudende."

In no ambiguous way the historical Confessions of Christendom testify against the idea of a "self-emptying" of Christ which involves any conversion or abandonment of divine attributes when the eternal Son of God became man. In line with this the older Reformed theologians used to speak of the kenosis of Christ not as *amissio, depositio* or *abditio* but as *occultatio* or *suppressio* of the divine attributes of Christ during His earthly life.

For an exhaustive treatment of the subject and relevant literature, especially in post-Reformation times, see Jac. J. Müller, *Die kenosisleer in die christologie sedert die Reformasie* (diss.), Amsterdam 1931.

8 This verse treats of Christ incarnate. In His outward form, in appearance and behaviour, in all His doings and actions, He was man like others. He was found in fashion as a man,[10] true man, and as man He humbled Himself. After the kenosis (emptying) of the *Logos asarkos* followed the *tapeinosis* (humiliation) of the *Logos ensarkos*. The whole time of His sojourn on earth was a time of self-humiliation. He was being humiliated and abased, instead of commanding and ruling in power and majesty and occupying a place of honour and authority and pre-eminence among men. From the manger to the cross He trod a path of humiliation, which culminated in the misery and suffering and reproach of a shameful death on a tree. Obedience unto God and surrender and submission to the will of God was maintained by Him unto the end, and the profoundest degree of humiliation was reached in that His death was not to be a natural or an honourable one, but was the painful and accursed death of the cross (cf. Deut. 21:23; Gal. 3:13).

---

[10] The previous expressions (with λαβών and γενόμενος) referred to the incarnation itself, and described the kenosis of Christ. Here Paul treats of Christ incarnate, Christ become man, and σχῆμα indicates the outer form or appearance in which the ὁμοίωμα ἀνθρώπων must find expression.

THE EXALTATION OF CHRIST AND HIS
RECOGNITION AS LORD

2:9—11

> 9 Wherefore also God highly exalted him, and gave unto him the name which is above every name;
>
> 10 that in the name of Jesus every knee should bow, of things in heaven and things on earth and things under the earth,
>
> 11 and that every tongue should confess that Jesus Christ is Lord, to the glory of God the Father.

9 After—and because of—His self-emptying and self-humiliation Christ experienced His exaltation by God.[1] Christ was highly (to the fullest extent) exalted by His resurrection from death, His ascension and investiture with power and majesty and glory. To Him the name[2] was given (literally: graciously given) by God, which is above every name. Paul does not state immediately what that name was, but from what follows later on, we can deduce that the highest of all names was that which indicated Christ's sovereign lordship, to wit the name Lord *(Kyrios)* a name in which is focussed His power and dignity, authority, honour and dominion, and worthiness of adoration. That Name is above every name borne by creatures in heaven and on earth.

10 The whole creation will pay homage and honour

---

[1] The idea of exaltation after humiliation often occurs in Scripture (Matt. 23:12; Luk. 14:11). Also Christ's exaltation is seen as fruit of His preceding humiliation.

[2] Although the reading ὄνομα is found in various old Mss., τὸ ὄνομα, supported by Aleph A B C, must have preference. *The name* (and not *a name*) is meant.

to the exalted Jesus. The "name of Jesus" signifies Jesus Himself. According to the Hebrew usage of the word, the *name* gives expression to the very being itself, and designates a person as he is, and as he reveals himself. It is remarkable that the Name at which every knee will have to bow is the name Jesus and no other, the appellation which denotes His earthly life and human nature, in which He came in the form of a servant for the salvation of the world. It is before Him who was exalted and glorified in His human nature, that every knee is to bow in acknowledgement and awe, in homage and adoration and worship. The whole creation, all rational beings, are classified in three groups here (cf. Rev. 5:13): first of all, the heavenly beings, the angels, or in a broader sense, the whole world of spirits (cf. Eph. 6:12); then the inhabitants of the earth, earthly beings, the living people on earth; and finally those who are under the earth, by which is meant the deceased souls, those who have "descended" into Hades.

The view that not only the rational creation is meant, but also the irrational,[3] every animate and inanimate creature (as Lightfoot suggests), cannot be maintained. Although

---

[3] The three adjectives ἐπουρανίων, ἐπιγείων and καταχθονίων, in their genitive form, can be taken either as masculine or as neuter, i.e. either in the sense of *those who are* ... or: *the things that are* in heaven, on earth and under the earth. In the latter case the irrational and inanimate creation could be included. The most plausible view, however, is that we have the masculine inflexion here, and that only the rational creation— the world of spirits and man—is meant. The bowing of the knee and the confession of the tongue point in that direction, and would be too strong metaphorical language to be used in connection with the inanimate and irrational creation. Only in very poetical or lyrical parts of Scripture, as in Ps. 148 or in Ps. 98:8, we find natural creation personified.

Christ's work of salvation also had cosmic significance and spelt deliverance for the whole natural creation (cf. Rom. 8:19—22), yet here the rational creation seems to be meant, because only there a knee could be bent and a tongue could make confession, and only with them a conscious act of adoration unto Jesus could take place.

11 Every tongue should confess[4] that Jesus Christ is Lord: angels and demons, the living and the dead, the saved and the lost will acknowledge Him as Lord, will recognise His Lordship, and confess that He is Lord even as God Himself.[5] All contradiction will cease and all denial will end; and the general acknowledgement and confession that Jesus Christ is Lord, will advance the glory of the Father who exalted Him and bestowed on Him that name. In this also the glorification of the Father is the ultimate purpose of all things.

---

[4] It is difficult to choose here between the reading ἐξομολογήσεται (fut. ind.), supported by A C D F G K L P, and the reading of Aleph and B, ἐξομολογήσηται (aor. subj.). The latter, however, is in agreement with the preceding κάμψῃ.

[5] κύριος does not necessarily denote deity or divinity, for it is also used of people (Col. 4:1, Eph. 6:9) in the sense of lord or master, to indicate their position of authority and lordship. Yet in connection with the Name of Jesus the word seems to point definitely to His divinity. As the exalted Saviour He is the divine *Kyrios*. Cf. Kittel, TWNT, III, 1041 and 1087 ff.

2:12—13

> 12 So then, my beloved, even as ye have always obeyed, not as in my presence only, but now much more in my absence, work out your own salvation with fear and trembling;
>
> 13 for it is God who worketh in you both to will and to work, for his good pleasure.

12 After this "Christ hymn" (verses 6—11), so striking and rich in contents, Paul reverts to the church with a word of exhortation with regard to their calling as believers, and thereby continues the admonition of verses 2—5,[1] which was interrupted by his reference to the perfect example of Christ. Believers are now called to self-activity by virtue of God's powerful working in them.

The church, his "beloved", (which manifests the intimate connection which bound Paul to his fellow-believers in Philippi), always showed obedience in the past[2] to Paul and his instructions and admonition, and are now exhorted to work out their own salvation, not only when the apostle is present with them,[3] but much more now that he is absent.

---

1 With the conjunction "so then" the verse is connected with the idea expressed in the first section of this chapter, but it can refer even further back to the admonition of 1:27: "Let your manner of life be worthy of the gospel ... whether I come and see you or be absent ..."

2 The phrase "not as in my presence only, but now much more in my absence" does not go with ὑπακούσατε preceding it (as if there was more obedience now, in the apostle's absence than in his presence), but with the principal verb of the sentence κατεργάζεσθε.

3 The addition of ὡς to μή, in the meaning of *as* or *as if*, evidently refers to a motive which could play a part with the Philippians, viz.

In his absence they have to apply themselves with even greater diligence and vigilance to the task of taking heed unto themselves and their spiritual well-being, and have to work out their salvation "with fear and trembling", i.e. conscious of their own insignificance and weakness and sinfulness and fallibility, and full of trembling and holy fear before God whose will is to be done, and for whose honour they have to work, and to whom an account will have to be given. To "work out" one's own[4] eternal welfare or salvation does not mean that man can or must work and accomplish it himself, for God does that (verse 13); but that the believer must finish, must carry to conclusion, must apply to its fullest consequences what is already given by God in principle. The believer is called to self-activity, to the active pursuit of the will of God, to the promotion of the spiritual life in himself, to the realisation of the virtues of the Christian life, and to a personal application of salvation. He must "work out" what God in His grace has "worked in".

13 The apostle gives his reason for this exhortation: "For it is God who worketh in you, both to will and to work, for (or better: for the sake of)[5] His good pleasure."

---

that they would do it only in Paul's presence or on account of his presence with them. In B and a few minuscules ὡς is omitted, which makes the meaning simpler.

4   ἑαυτῶν and not ἀλλήλων: your *own* and not that of one another. The concern is always with one's own salvation, in spite of one's concern for the interests of others. Interest in the spiritual welfare of others should not result in the neglect of one's own spiritual welfare and salvation. One should go on uninterruptedly making provision for one's own soul.

5   ὑπέρ is best translated by for, for the sake of, in execution of, in the interest of. The meaning of the verse is: It is God who, in the

Their salvation is, therefore, in the first instance, the work of God, not of themselves, and all spiritual life and demonstration of power in them is the fruit of the grace of God. And because this all is the work of God, the redeemed can in no other way "work out" their own salvation than with fear and trembling before God. This powerful inward working of God affects both the will and the work, the decision of the will and the practical deed. To will and to do is the fruit of God's work in the believer (cf. Eph. 2:8, John 15:5) for the sake of and towards the execution of God's good pleasure and His eternal decree. The good pleasure of God is free and sovereign; and where He, in executing His good pleasure, is mightily at work in the believer towards his salvation, this at the same time also demands the self-activity of man, in working out that salvation to His honour and glorification. So divine sovereignty and human responsibility time and again meet each other in the life of the redeemed.

---

execution of His good pleasure (for, or for the sake of His good pleasure), works in you both to will and to work.

2:14—18

14 Do all things without murmurings and questionings:

15 that ye may become blameless and harmless, children of God without blemish in the midst of a crooked and perverse generation, among whom ye are seen as lights in the world,

16 holding forth the word of life; that I may have whereof to glory in the day of Christ, that I did not run in vain neither labor in vain.

17 Yea, and if I am offered upon the sacrifice and service of your faith, I joy, and rejoice with you all:

18 and in the same manner do ye also joy, and rejoice with me.

14 In working out their salvation (verse 12) the church must do all that lies in the path of Christian calling and Christian duty without discontent with and grumbling against the will and decrees and claims of God. This will demand self-denial and self-renunciation (verses 3 and 4), and may bring along suffering (1:29) and also the temptation to raise all kinds of objections and arguments and criticism. There must be no opposition or questioning with them who wish to carry into effect the calling of God for their lives.

15 For with believers an outwardly blameless life must couple itself with inward sincerity and purity and simplicity. Those who belong to Christ must be[1] children of God

---

[1] γένησθε, **in contrast with the static** ἦτε (as with A D F G), **denotes** rather the process of becoming, of realising what is pursued.

without blemish or defect[2]; otherwise there is still so much in them that is defective and imperfect, so many shortcomings which are inconsistent with their high calling and the saintly conduct which is expected of the children of God. In the midst of[3] a "crooked and perverse generation", among people who do not keep straight, who hold wrong views, who follow a distorted way of life, deviating from the norms contained in the Word of God, believers have the calling to be different, to be God's children without blemish, and to be seen[4] as lights or light-bearers[5] in the world (cf. Eph. 5:8; Matt. 5:14).

16 They can be such lights or spreaders of light because they themselves possess the word of life, the word of salvation which is life and which gives life (John 6:63; Rom. 1:18), but also because they hold out its light in front of them, as it were, towards others.[6] The believers as bearers

---

2 "ἄμεμπτοι relates to the judgment of others, while ἀκέραιοι describes the intrinsic character" (Lightfoot). ἀκέραιος means sincere, pure, unmixed (from κεράννυμι = mix).

3 μέσον used adverbially instead of ἐν μέσῳ (T.R.).

4 φαίνεσθε (med.) does not actually mean "shine" (RSV) (as the active φαίνετε does), but appear, be revealed. It can be taken as indicative or imperative. Although the latter is not impossible (and is even preferred by some scholars, including Greijdanus, who views this word as coloured to a large extent by the imperative of verse 14, and accordingly translates: "among whom you must be seen as lights"), the indicative nevertheless seems to be the more natural construction.

5 φωστῆρες (lights) really means stars, bearers of light. "Zunächst der Lichtträger, und dann das Licht selbst," Str.-B. III, p. 621.

6 ἐπέχειν does not, strictly speaking, mean to have, to possess, to hold fast, but considering the force of the prefix ἐπι-: to hold before, to hold out to others, to hold forth, like a torch which is held out before the bearer.

of light hold fast the word of life and make it shine before the world through their sincere disposition and exemplary conduct. The world hears the word from them, but also sees its light in their daily walk of life; their saintly lives testify to the power of the word of life.

Paul himself also had an interest in the testimony coming forth from the life of the believers, for they were the fruit of his labour among them. If their faith was genuine and pure and without blemish, and the light of grace was seen in them, he would not stand ashamed but would find in it a reason to be proud in the day of Christ, i.e. His advent, when his apostolic labour would be weighed and judged.

Then it would be evident that the labour carried on in Christ's Name with exertion of all his powers was not in vain, and that he did not run in vain.[7] Paul ran hard in the race of the gospel, but he won; he laboured hard for the cause of the gospel, but the fruit thereof did not fail. Faithful devotion to the task allotted to him would ultimately be rewarded.

17–18 Something more, however, than running and labouring on behalf of the church is possible. In addition thereto Paul may be called to lay down his life. Together with the sacrifice and service offered by the Philippians it may still be found necessary that the life of the apostle be poured forth as a libation.[8] Their faith had already brought

---

[7] The idea of a race in the stadium is expressed here. (Cf. Gal. 2:2; 1 Cor. 9:24; 2 Tim. 4:7).

[8] $\dot{\epsilon}\pi\dot{\iota}$ can be understood here in the sense of *upon* or *with*. With the heathen sacrificial customs a libation was poured out upon or over the sacrificial offering; with the Jewish sacrificial cult the libation was poured out (not upon the sacrifice but) next to or around the altar

its sacrificial offering and rendered its service[9] to the cause of God; there had already been sacrifices and suffering on the part of believers for the sake of Christ and His cause (cf. 1:28, 29). They had already laid themselves down as a sacrifice on the altar of consecration to God and His service. In addition to and upon that offering, Paul's life can still be poured forth as an accompanying libation.

But even if that should happen, there is cause for rejoicing, for it will be to the honour of God and for the welfare of the church and in the interest of Christ's cause on earth. Indeed, Christ will be magnified "whether by life or by death" (1:20). The apostle, together with[10] the church is glad because of their faith which offers and serves; such powerful and devoted life can be only a cause of rejoicing to all of them. He therefore[11] exhorts them to rejoice on account of their living and active faith, and to be glad together with him, the apostle, who collaborated thereunto by his preaching of the gospel to them. "I am glad—be ye also glad; I with you and you with me."

---

on which the sacrifice was laid. In any case, the death of Paul is considered as an additional sacrifice to that of the Philippians.

9 λειτουργία means: service to God or His cause; or manner of divine worship. The word is also used to denote any priestly action or sacred performance, and in a worldly sense to denote a service to the state or to the public. Cf. Cremer, *op. cit.*, pp. 761—3; Kittel, TWNT, IV, pp. 223 and 232 ff.

10 συγχαίρω with the meaning of congratulate (so Meyer, Lightfoot) does not make good sense here. There is sufficient reason to take it in the sense of "to rejoice with."

11 τὸ δὲ αὐτό means: for the same reason, just so, likewise, and is used adverbially in the sense of ὡσαύτως.

2:19—24

19 But I hope in the Lord Jesus to send Timothy shortly unto you, that I also may be of good comfort, when I know your state.

20 For I have no man likeminded, who will care truly for your state.

21 For they all seek their own, not the things of Jesus Christ.

22 But ye know the proof of him, that, as a child serveth a father, so he served with me in furtherance of the gospel.

23 Him therefore I hope to send forthwith, so soon as I shall see how it will go with me:

24 but I trust in the Lord that I myself also shall come shortly.

19 Although Paul cannot be with the church at present, he hopes to send Timothy to them soon and to be able to come to them himself eventually (verse 24). His hope is "in the Lord Jesus" (for the expression see also 1:14, 2:24, 3:1), and has its ground in his fellowship with Christ. His thoughts, intentions, desires and hope flow fortlı from his mystical union with Christ. By the apostle's use of the appellation "Lord Jesus"[1] instead of the more usual "Christ Jesus" he possibly intends to accentuate the idea of Christ's will and lordship and right of disposal over all the apostle's doings, intentions and expectations. The Lord would lead and dispose and decide in these matters.

---

[1] Although Paul uses this expression frequently, as a rule, however, we find that he uses the name: Christ Jesus. C D F and G have here, apparently by way of correction, the reading ἐν χριστῷ.

Timothy is not only sent to them,[2] but for them and on their behalf, for their good; thereby Paul himself also will be cheered and encouraged, for Timothy will not only encourage them by his reports concerning Paul and the cause of Christ in Rome, but returning will be able to encourage Paul with reassuring and comforting tidings concerning the church and the progress of the gospel among them. Through Timothy, his fellow worker, Paul will then hear of all the circumstances of the church at Philippi.

20-21 Timothy, to be sure, is being sent, because Paul has nobody like him (literally: of like mind),[3] who will look after and attend to the interests of the church in such a genuine and upright manner. For all the others (and here we must suppose Mark and Luke as probably absent from Rome at the time), the whole circle of brothers around him, do not put the cause of Christ in the foreground in such a way and with such self-forgetful devotion, that he can send them; with them personal consideration and their own interests[4] carry greater weight than the sacrifices on behalf of the cause of Christ. They lack the right spirit and disposition, and are therefore unfit to carry out the task.

22-24 Timothy, on the other hand, is a well-tried and

---

2 ὑμῖν and not πρὸς ὑμᾶς (as D has it) is the correct reading, and does not so much mean *to you* as *for you*.

3 ἰσόψυχος is a *hapax legomenon* in the N. T. With it αὐτῷ must be understood as complement, and not μοι (as Vincent suggests), for thereby an unintended comparison would be made between Timothy and Paul.

4 A fatiguing journey to Macedonia, the responsibility of the task that had to be undertaken, personal business that required attention, or mere selfishness and indolence and self-sufficiency—such things could make their own interests carry greater weight than the cause of Christ. "O quam multi sua causa pii sunt!" (Bengel).

worthy servant of the Lord. He proved himself fit and trustworthy. He stood the test and his virtue was proved.[5] As the spiritual child of Paul (cf. 1 Tim. 1:2; 2 Tim. 1:2) he served him with devotion and subservience, and at the same time[6] stood with him as a fellow servant of Jesus Christ on behalf of[7] and for the expansion of the gospel. Paul is hoping to send Timothy without delay, as soon as he has seen how things will go with him, and as soon as the course which events take and the issue become clearer to him. And not only does he hope to send Timothy immediately, but he confidently expects to come soon himself. This trust and good expectation are also "in the Lord" (cf. verse 19), grounded in the will and wishes and permission of Christ, and experienced in intimate communion of life with Christ.

---

[5] $\delta o\varkappa\iota\mu\acute{\eta}$ may mean: a test, the process of testing and trying, or (as here) the result of testing, the worth or proved reliability.

[6] "A mixed construction ... Paul first thinks of Timothy as his son in the gospel, serving him with a son's devotion. But before the sentence is finished, his lowliness reminds him that they are both alike servants of a common Lord, equal in His sight" (Kennedy, Exp. Gr. Test. ad hoc.).

[7] $\varepsilon\iota\varsigma$ here means: with a view to, in the interest of, for the expansion of. Timothy did not only assist Paul in founding the church at Philippi (Acts 16), but also paid other visits there together with Paul (Acts 20).

CONCERNING EPAPHRODITUS AND HIS RETURN
TO PHILIPPI

2:25—30

25 But I counted it necessary to send to you Epaphroditus, my brother and fellow-worker and fellow-soldier, and your messenger and minister to my need;

26 since he longed after you all, and was sore troubled, because ye had heard that he was sick:

27 for indeed he was sick nigh unto death: but God had mercy on him; and not on him only, but on me also, that I might not have sorrow upon sorrow.

28 I have sent him therefore the more diligently, that, when ye see him again, ye may rejoice, and that I may be the less sorrowful.

29 Receive him therefore in the Lord with all joy; and hold such in honor:

30 because for the work of Christ he came nigh unto death, hazarding his life to supply that which was lacking in your service toward me.

25 Paul hopes to send Timothy to Philippi shortly, and trusts that he himself will soon follow, but meanwhile sends back to them Epaphroditus,[1] the church's messenger to him. He regards this mission as necessary and urgent. Epaphroditus was sent to Paul by the church with their gift (4:18), and is now sent back, probably also as the bearer of this Letter to the church. He is described here by various

---

[1] Epaphroditus is only known to us from this verse and from 4:18. Epaphras, also a fellow worker of Paul who associated with him during his imprisonment (Col. 1:7, 4:12, Philemon 23), is not the same person. Epaphras comes from Colossae, while Epaphroditus is from Philippi.

names. He is Paul's "brother" in the faith and fellow Christian, his "fellow-worker" in the cause of the gospel, and also his "fellow-soldier" in the fight against the powers of the Evil One and the enemies of the cross. There is fellowship with Paul in faith, in work and in the fight. Furthermore, Epaphroditus is the church's messenger (literally: apostle),[2] a delegate sent with a special commission, and also their "minister[3] to my need," who in bringing the gift to the ambassador of God in captivity, performed a sacred service.

26–28 The reason why the apostle deems it necessary to send Epaphroditus is to be sought in the latter's very fervent longing[4] for all the saints there. Another factor however was his concern and distress[5] because the Philippians had heard that he had taken ill[6] after his arrival in Rome and were anxious and worried about his condition. Paul confirms the report that Epaphroditus had indeed

---

2 ἀπόστολος here does not denote the special office of apostle as held by the twelve, but is the general name and designation of a person sent or commissioned as delegate of the church.

3 The idea of "sacrificial minister" (Meyer, Lightfoot, Vincent, Kennedy), one who performs a sacred service, is supported by 4:18, where the gift brought to Paul by Epaphroditus is called an offering (θυσία).

4 A fervent longing is expressed by ἐπιποθῶν. Aleph A C D E insert ἰδεῖν after ἐπιποθῶν, probably to bring it in line with instances like Rom. 1:11, 2 Tim. 1:4.

5 ἀδημονεῖν is probably derived from α— and δῆμος, with the meaning of: away from home or people, and metaphorically: not inwardly at home, beside oneself, anxious, distressed.

6 ἠσθένησεν must be regarded as aor. ingress. with the meaning of: *became* ill (and not: *was* ill). The news that he took ill became known at Philippi and caused great anxiety. The church had to be reassured by news of his recovery.

been very ill, near to death, but that it was a thing of the past now by the grace of God. God had mercy on him by healing and restoring him to health. At the same time God was also merciful to Paul in healing Epaphroditus, so that he should not have one sorrow after another, first on account of his illness and possibly later on on account of his death. Paul was therefore eager to send[7] him back to the church, so that they, seeing him healthy and well in their midst, might rejoice again after the anxiety they endured on his account. So also Paul himself could be less sorrowful (literally: more unsorrowful), knowing that Epaphroditus had arrived safely among them again and that there was no more reason whatever left for any further anxiety.

29-30 The church is exhorted to receive Epaphroditus "in the Lord," in gratitude towards the Lord and in the knowledge that he had been restored to them by the Lord, and with heartfelt joy. In addition they were to honour with respect and high esteem men of such caliber. For he carried out the work of Christ[8] with all that it demanded in the way of sacrifice and privation, and even risked his life[9] and came near to death by the serious illness he con-

---

[7] ἔπεμψα must be taken as an epistolary aorist, and the sentence translated: "I send him the more eagerly (speedily)". When the letter was received by the church, the sending of Epaphroditus would, however, already be a matter of the past.

[8] Here we have a number of variants. B F G have τὸ ἔργον χριστοῦ, with D E K L nearly the same, viz. τὸ ἔργον τοῦ χριστοῦ, while Aleph A P have τὸ ἔργον κυρίου. κυρίου for χριστοῦ may be due to an unintentional error of the ear or memory, or to an intentional equalisation with the expression as found in 1 Cor. 15:58, 16:10, etc.

[9] Literally translated: gambled with his soul. παραβουλευσάμενος with C K L P does not give good sense, and can be explained as a

tracted while he was busy completing the service of the church to the apostle. This lack or deficiency in the service (which again is considered as a sacred and priestly ministry, cf. verses 17 and 25) was due evidently to the fact that the church itself could not assist or serve Paul in his captivity. But this service Epaphroditus could now supplement and complete by his presence and personal care for the apostle. Such self-forgetful work of charity, wrought even at the risk of his own health, was indeed a sacred ministry and consecrated service.

---

variant for the less known παραβολευσάμενος which means: to risk, to gamble, to stake.

CHAPTER III

WARNING AGAINST JUDAISTIC TEACHERS

3:1—3

1 Finally, my brethren, rejoice in the Lord. To write the same things to you, to me indeed is not irksome, but for you it is safe.

2 Beware of the dogs, beware of the evil workers, beware of the concision:

3 for we are the circumcision, who worship by the Spirit of God, and glory in Christ Jesus, and have no confidence in the flesh:

1 The chapter begins[1] with an exhortation to rejoice. It is a call which is heard several times in the Letter (2:18; 4:4; cf. also 1:4, 1:8, 1:25), and is directed to his "brethren," which is a manner of address expressing an intimate fellowship in the faith (cf. also 4:1). A divine joy in the Lord is possible for the believer in spite of adversities, struggles or difficulties. He can rejoice *in the Lord*—in His fellowship, in His love and grace, and in the knowledge of His dominion over our lives and His rule over all our destinies.

But there is something else to which the apostle—once again—wishes to draw their attention. He wants "to write the same things" to them, and therewith refers to what is

---

[1] The expression τὸ λοιπόν (meaning furthermore, for the rest, finally) could already be considered as an indication of the approaching conclusion of the Letter. Cf. 2 Cor. 13:11, Eph. 6:10, 1 Thess. 4:1. Paul, however, immediately after this follows a long detour, namely to treat of the Judaizers and to draw attention to the attitude that befits the true Christian.

being dealt with in the following few verses, namely the Judaistic infection—a matter about which Paul had written to the churches before now (cf. the Letter to the Galatians). This he had undoubtedly also already mentioned to the church at Philippi,[2] because it was of general occurrence and constituted an actual and perilous phenomenon in the early Christian churches. Now he is going to treat the subject pertinently in writing again. It is a repeated warning against the false teachers of Judaism, an exhortation which will serve to promote the security and safety of the church, and so to express it again is not irksome to the apostle. "Repeated warning can prevent our losing sight of the danger and rouses us to continuous watchfulness ... It prevents negligence and thus promotes safety" (Greijdanus).

2 "Beware of" (look, take heed!) is repeated three times

---

[2] Different interpretations are offered for τὰ αὐτὰ γράφειν: (a) that it alludes to earlier oral communications to the Philippians by Paul (so Beza, Erasmus, Calvin. The latter puts it this way: "Eadem repetere quae praesens dixeram"); (b) that it refers to a letter formerly written to the Philippians but which got lost. (Thus Zahn, Meyer, Vincent, Barth, with reference also to the word of Polycarp in his Letter to the Philippians (3, 2) that the apostle ἀπὼν ὑμῖν ἔγραψεν ἐπιστολάς. See Introduction. Cf. also Lightfoot on: "Lost Epistles to the Philippians," in Comm., p. 138); (c) that it refers to the exhortation, immediately preceding in this Letter, to rejoice in the Lord, and that it is this matter that is repeated once more, cf. 1:4; 2:17, 18; 2:28, 29. (So Alford and Weiss). It is, however, a very improbable solution, because the clause "it is safe for you" (that is, it provides certainty) at the conclusion of the verse refers to a preceding *warning* or indication of danger, and does not fit in with the exhortation to rejoice.

The questions that arise here are: When did Paul on an earlier occasion treat of these "same" things, and what were they? Was the earlier communication in connection with them oral or written? If the latter, did it happen in this present Letter or somewhere else?

with an urgent insistence. It is a very real menace to the Christian Church against which this warning is uttered. Dogs—evilworkers—mutilators of the flesh: with these three appellations the false teachers and seducers are described. We surely need not (with B. Weiss) see three categories of people in this, viz. heathen, self-seeking Christian teachers, and Jews. It is one kind of false teacher which is portrayed from three different angles. Thereby, moreover, not the same persons as in chapter 1:15—18 are meant. For there Paul described Christian teachers who preached Christ, but with impure motives, people who were pro-Christ but anti-Paul, and therefore preached Christ from envy and strife and rivalry. Here probably the point at issue is a distortion of the Christian gospel, a denial of the sufficiency of the work of Christ. From the context (verses 2—3, 6—7) it appears that Judaizers are meant here, who suggested that circumcision of the flesh was indispensable for the attainment of righteousness before God, and who based their hope of salvation on circumcision and the fulfilment of the law and not exclusively on Christ's work of redemption. "Dogs" is an expression of reproach and contempt, probably on account of the impurity and irksomeness and impudence of these creatures.[3] "The herds of dogs which prowl about Eastern cities, without a home and without an owner, feeding on the refuse and filth of the streets, quarrelling among themselves, and attacking the passer-by, explain the

---

[3] The dog was generally considered by the Jews as "das verachtetste, frechste und elendeste Geschöpf" (the most despised, shameless and miserable creature), Str.-Billerbeck I, 722. Cf. also III. 621. This word which was used by the Jews contemptuously with regard to all Gentiles, the ceremonial impure (cf. the allusion in Matt. 15:27), is now used against the Judaizers themselves.

applications of the image" (Lightfoot). Next to this expression of contempt the term "evil-workers" is used to denote that their zeal and labour were directed toward the distortion and perversion of the pure doctrine of justification by faith. It was destructive work rather than upbuilding of the faith of the church. Together with that the Judaizers, with a play of words on "circumcision," are ridiculed as the "concision" (mutilation or cutting in pieces). With them circumcision is not a matter of the heart, but merely concision or mutilation of the flesh. Although they profess to believe in Christ, they boast of the circumcision of the body and its value towards righteousness before God, and they demand circumcision from all confessors of Christ (cf. Acts 15:1). To Paul such action is worthless mutilation of the flesh, and something which denies the all-sufficiency of Christ. (Cf. Gal. 5:2—6; 1 Cor. 7:18—19).

3 In avowed opposition to this, Paul bears witness to the nature of the true circumcision. The true circumcision is something inward and consists in the discarding of the impurity and the insensitiveness of the heart (cf. Rom. 2:25—29; Col. 2:11). The circumcision of the flesh alone is no true circumcision. But all who believe in Christ and serve in the Spirit of God, have undergone the true circumcision.

Three characteristics of the truly circumcised are successively stated. Firstly they are people who "worship by the Spirit of God",[4] i.e. inwardly renewed through and

---

[4] The translation here ought to be: "We who worship by the Spirit of God" instead of: "We who worship God in spirit" (RSV), or: "We who worship God in the spirit" (AV). λατρεύειν in Scripture generally denotes the worship *of God,* or divine worship. Cf. Cremer, *Bibl.-theol. Wörterbuch,* p. 389.

empowered by the Spirit of God, people who live by and serve through His Spirit. Furthermore, they are people who "glory in Christ Jesus" and His perfect work of redemption as the only ground of their salvation, and do not boast of personal goodness or works or deserts. Christ receives all the honour and His Name alone is magnified. From this it ultimately follows that they are people who "have no confidence in the flesh." This refers of course to the circumcision of the flesh in which the Judaizers put their trust but which the true Christian does not trust for his salvation. But to Paul "flesh" also has a wider meaning[5] and can be understood to mean "self," the "carnal man," the works of the "old nature," on which man sometimes puts his trust: physical, intellectual, spiritual, ceremonial works and privileges which are carnal and which stand in contrast with the Spirit of God and His works.

The concision or "mutilation" trusts in the flesh, the true "circumcision" trusts only in Jesus Christ.

---

[5] In addition to the literal meaning of "flesh" as the matter or substance of which the body consists, or the material body itself, the word is also used in a moral sense, to denote the sinful way of living of mankind, natural man in his sinful and unregenerate state and inclinations, in contrast with the "spirit": man turned towards God under the inspiration of the Holy Spirit. For the different meanings of the word, see, G. B. Stevens, *Theol. of N. T.*, Rev. Ed., pp. 338—348; Cremer, *Bibl.-Theol. Lex.*, pp. 852—856; *Christelijke Encyclopaedie* V, art. "Vleesch bij Paulus."

PAUL'S GROUND FOR CONFIDENCE IN THE FLESH

3:4—6

4 though I myself might have confidence even in the flesh:
if any other man thinketh to have confidence in the flesh,
I yet more:

5 circumcised the eighth day, of the stock of Israel, of the
tribe of Benjamin, a Hebrew of Hebrews; as touching the
law, a Pharisee;

6 as touching zeal, persecuting the church; as touching the
righteousness which is in the law, found blameless.

4 Paul is no stranger to the various privileges which
could give him a reason for glorying in the flesh and for
putting his trust therein.[1] More than anybody else, more
than any of the Judaizers themselves, he could have trusted
in the flesh and carnal privileges, namely the privileges and
advantages which he as a Jew enjoyed, and which he now
mentions by name.

5-6 He was "circumcised on the eighth day": in this,
as a child of the covenant, he was treated at the appointed
time according to the instructions of God (Gen. 17:2,
Lev. 12:3). He is "of the people of Israel": born of the
people of the Covenant as a true Israelite, and therefore
not a proselyte from the gentiles. He is "of the tribe of
Benjamin":[2] his descent is more closely described as from
that tribe which gave the first king to the Kingdom of

---

[1] πεποίθησις must not be understood here in the subjective sense
as *confidence* (this Paul no longer had in the flesh after his conversion),
but in the objective sense of: *ground* or *reason for confidence*.

[2] Benjamin was the beloved youngest son of Jacob, born of Rachel
in the land of Canaan (Gen. 35:16—18).

Israel (1 Sam. 9), the tribe which remained faithful, together with Judah, to the Davidic royal house, and in whose territory Jerusalem lay (Judges 1:21). He is "a Hebrew of Hebrews";[3] although born in the diaspora (Tarsus), he is of pure Jewish descent, and maintains his Jewish language and customs and manner of life; he is no Hellenist or Graecised Jew, and, born of Pharisaic parents (Acts 23:6), he is also educated in Jerusalem in the law and morals of his fathers, and in Hebrew, his mother tongue. He can therefore trace his genealogy as a full-blooded Jew.

Furthermore, he was "as to the law a Pharisee", a member of the most strict and law-abiding sect of Judaism, the orthodox defenders of the Mosaic Law, who stood firm by the traditions of the fathers and were held in high esteem by the people. He was a disciple, admirer and passionate adherent of the strictest religious tradition among the Jews (cf. Gal. 1:14). As to "zeal" he was, "persecuting the Church".[4] His zeal for the law and the protection of the

---

3 Hebrews are, according to Acts 6:1, the Hebrew-speaking Jews in contrast with the Greek-speaking Jews or Hellenists. Paul designates himself as "Hebräisch (Aramäisch) redender Jude von Hebr. (Aram.) redenden Juden," Str.-B. III, 622. Cf. also Kittel III, p. 392 ff.

"Within the pale of the Jewish Church a man was Ἰουδαῖος, who traced his descent from Jacob and conformed to the religion of his fathers, but he was not Ἑβραῖος also, unless he spoke the Hebrew tongue and retained Hebrew customs" (Lightfoot, ad loc.).

4 The word ἐκκλησία, derived from ἐκ-καλεῖν, has ungone various changes of meaning. (a) In classical Greek it denoted a national convention or public assembly to which the citizens or inhabitants had been called together. (In the N. T. it is used once in this sense, viz. Acts 19:39); (b) In the LXX it has the meaning of an assembly of the people of Israel called together (1 Kings 8:65), and it is alternated with συναγωγή. It already begins to be used in connection with the

Jewish religion drove him even to the persecution and extermination of the church of God at Jerusalem and elsewhere. His blind hatred against Christ and the Church showed how completely he was devoured by his zeal for the Jewish cause. He was ready to go to the utmost against the church and the confessors of Christ in general. Finally he could also boast that he was "blameless" as to "righteousness which is in the law." As regards his righteousness, obedience to and conformity with the demands of God for his life, there was nothing to be brought in against him. It was, however, a righteousness "in the law", i.e. it sought its norm and measure in the literal and outward observance of the law and in obedience to the formal dictates thereof. In those respects his righteousness was without blemish and according to human opinion irreproachable. Conduct and manner of life, ceremonial and moral relation to the law, left nothing to be desired.

Religion, race, descent, national attachment, conscientious Pharisaic observance of the law, fervent zeal and blameless outward righteousness—all were in his favour, if he wished to put his confidence in the flesh. But Christ became a reality in his life, and his assessment of the value of things would undergo a radical change.

---

religious. (c) In the N. T. it is used in a religious sense for the congregation or community of all who are called by and to Christ, who confess Him and are participators of His salvation: i.e. the congregation or church (Acts 2:47, Gal. 1:13, Phil. 3:6, cf. also Matt. 16:18). It is also used for the local or individual revelation of the catholic Church, viz. the separate or particular congregation or church (Rom. 16:5, 1 Cor. 1:2, Col. 4:15). Cf. Cremer, *op. cit.*, p. 322, and Kittel, TWNT, III, 505 ff.

3:7—11

7 Howbeit what things were gain to me, these have I counted loss for Christ.

8 Yea verily, and I count all things to be loss for the excellency of the knowledge of Christ Jesus my Lord: for whom I suffered the loss of all things, and do count them but refuse, that I may gain Christ,

9 and be found in him, not having a righteousness of mine own, even that which is of the law, but that which is through faith in Christ, the righteousness which is from God by faith:

10 that I may know him, and the power of his resurrection, and the fellowship of his sufferings, becoming conformed unto his death;

11 if by any means I may attain unto the resurrection from the dead.

7 A very significant howbeit[1] now follows, which depicts the all-changing "Umwertung aller Werte" (revaluing of all values) in the life of the apostle. The things that were gain to him, the carnal advantages and privileges in which he could put confidence—religion, race and descent, law-observance, zeal and outward blamelessness—are now, for the sake of Christ, regarded[2] as loss and even harm, as a result of the absolute transformation his life had undergone. Christ made all the difference. The things he formerly

---

[1] ἀλλὰ is omitted by Codd. Aleph and A, but is supported by B D any many other Mss.

[2] The perfect form of the verb denotes a lasting condition which began in the past. The meaning here is: "I counted it as loss and am still counting it as such."

112

cherished as valuable, appeared not only worthless, but even harmful. "It is not Nil that takes the place of the former Plus, but the Plus itself is changed to a Minus" (Barth). In the light of Christ Paul sees the guilt, wrong and reject-ableness of the supposed "irreproachable life" of Pharisaic righteousness, and how it endangered the soul's salvation.[3]

8 It was no passing impulse when at his conversion he counted those things loss which were gain to him. It became a lasting attitude[4] or way of life. "I counted" of the past is continued by "I count" in the present. And now nothing whatsoever is excluded. All things are subordinated and counted as loss because of the all-surpassing worth of the personally experienced saving knowledge of Jesus Christ (cf. John 17:3), whom the apostle furthermore qualifies as "my Lord", by which he gives expression to his personal relationship to Christ, whom he learned to know as the Glorified and the *Kyrios,* and whom he confesses as the Lord of *his* life. For His sake Paul was ready at his con-version to lose and to abandon all things which had value for him; he suffered the loss "even of esteem and friend-ship and enjoyment and rest and relations" (Greijdanus);

---

[3] Greijdanus here suggests the figure of a ship with a valuable freight, which is compelled to throw overboard in stormy weather those valuable articles which were counted as gain, in order to save the ship and life on board (cf. Acts 27:17, 38 as a case in point)— valuable articles which, however, are in the way now, and must be cast away as dangerous.

[4] The first clause is not easily translated on account of the number or particles. ἀλλά is used here with intensifying force, not in contrast with what precedes. "Yes, indeed, also," "Yes, truly, also," "Sure, even . . .," "Yea, doubtless" will more or less be a rendering of the five little words in the original.

and he counted all things (even now still) as refuse or dung[5]
—worthless and rejectable, unattractive and undesired, cast
away from him for good, "in order that he may gain Christ."
The former gain was rejected in order to obtain a better
gain. He could not have those things and also Christ.
Nothing together with Christ, was preferable to all things
without Christ. Christ Himself would henceforth be the
gain which would enrich his life.

9 The abandoning of what formerly was gain, would
furthermore have as result that he would obtain a new
righteousness. It would be found and would become
apparent that in Christ, i.e. by virtue of his fellowship and
union with Christ through faith, he no longer had a
righteousness of his own, "of the law", no longer a righteousness which consisted in the strict outward fulfilment
of the obligations of the law and was based on the
works of the law, no longer the law-observing Pharisaic
righteousness which characterised his previous life, but
instead a righteousness "through faith in Christ," a rightness
of attitude towards God accomplished by reason of the fact
that it was appropriated by way of faith in Christ. The contrast is now clearly drawn between the former righteousness
of the law and the new experience of righteousness *through
faith in Christ*.[6] The latter is more closely defined as "the

---

[5] It seems as if σκύβαλα is used with two meanings, although the
true derivation is uncertain, viz. (a) excrement from the body ; (b)
refuse or fragments remaining after a feast which are removed from
the table and thrown away (to the dogs?). Cf. Lightfoot, Comm.
ad loc.

[6] διὰ πίστεως denotes faith as a means, not as the ground or
cause working the righteousness, which would have been denoted by

righteousness which is from God by faith." God is the origin and source of it, while faith is the means or way or instrument by which it is appropriated. True righteousness is not worked by law or the observance of law, but is granted by God as a gift of grace and is accepted and personally appropriated by faith.[7] In Christ the believer is found with a righteousness which is from God—a justification by God for Christ's sake, the putting of man's life in the right relation to God, and the bringing about of a way of life which is righteous in the eye of God.

Nobody can, therefore, rely on a righteousness *from man* (based on law, acquired by virtue of his own conformity to the law), but only on a righteousness *from God,* appropriated through faith. Man can offer nothing acceptable *to God,* but all good things are granted him *by God* and are accepted through faith.

10-11 By counting all as loss and by gaining Christ (verse 8), and having obtained the righteousness from God through faith in Christ (verse 9), the apostle further aims at a more intimate and personal knowledge[8] and experience of Christ by reason of his union with Him in faith. He

---

διὰ πίστιν. In χριστοῦ we have an objective genitive depicting Christ as the object of the faith.

[7] "Fides offert nudum hominem Deo" (Calvin). Faith offers naked man to God. In him there is nothing good—he stands empty-handed—there is nothing in or on him to justify him before God. There can, therefore, never be a righteousness of his own, earned or acquired by man himself, *his own* righteousness. The only true righteousness is granted and imputed to man by God for the sake of Christ, and is accepted by man in faith.

[8] By γνῶναι (infinitive of purpose) not only intellectual knowledge is meant, but personal contact of life (cf. John 17:3).

115

desires to know Christ in the power of His resurrection and in the fellowship of His sufferings. By "the power of His resurrection"[9] is meant the living power which proceeds from the risen Saviour and reveals itself in the believer by working a total renewal of life in him. "It is the power of the risen Christ as it becomes a subject of practical knowledge and a power in Paul's inner life" (Vincent). Paul desires a deeply experienced knowledge of the living and life-giving Christ. That power of Christ's resurrection is evident in that "we have been raised together with Christ" (Col. 3:1), that God "even when we were dead through our trespasses, made us alive together with Christ" (Eph. 2:5, 6), and that "as Christ was raised from the dead ... we also might walk in newness of life" (Rom. 6:4).

The "fellowship of His sufferings" is the other experience of faith that results from the mystical union of the believer with Christ.[10] It follows on the experience of the power of Christ's resurrection—not the other way about—for first of all the believer shares in the *life* of the risen Lord, but after that also in His *sufferings*. This does not mean sharing the atoning and redemptive suffering of Christ on the cross, but it means a personal dying to sin (mortificatio), the crucifying of the flesh, and suffering for the sake of Christ and His cause. This fellowship in suffering is described

---

9 By "the power of His resurrection" is not meant here the power revealed in the historic resurrection of Christ on Easter, nor the power of Christ by which Paul also would experience a resurrection after death, but it refers to the power of the resurrected Christ which forms the principle of the new life in the regenerate and works towards the complete renewal of man.

10 "Being in Christ involves fellowship with Christ at all points—his life, his spirit, his sufferings, his death and his glory" (Vincent, *ad loc.*).

furthermore by the expression, "becoming conformed unto His death." This does not mean that the believer must die as Christ did, and if need be die on the cross; but the believer is "crucified with Christ" (Gal. 2:20), dies daily (1 Cor. 15:31), "always bearing about in the body the dying of Jesus" (2 Cor. 4:10), has been united with Christ "in the likeness of His death," for "the old man was crucified with Him that the body of sin might be done away, that so we should no longer be in bondage to sin" (Rom. 6:5, 6).

Sharing the sufferings of Christ is, therefore, more than just suffering for the sake of Christ (in tribulation and persecution), or in imitation of Christ. It means all suffering, bodily or spiritual,[11] which overtakes the believer by virtue of his new manner of life, his "Christ life" in a world unbelieving and hostile to Christ. "It implies all pangs and all afflictions undergone in the struggle against sin either within or without. The agony of Gethsemane, not less than the agony of Calvary, will be reproduced however faintly in the faithful servant of Christ" (Lightfoot).

The believer comes to knowledge and experience of this by his mystical fellowship with the living Christ.

The last expression "if by any means[12] I may attain unto

---

[11] "The nature of the suffering can be twofold: purely spiritual and inward as a struggle against and grief over sin in the heart, or otherwise outward and real, as privations owing to persecution or bodily pain in the struggle against the world" (Groenewald, *Koinonia by Paulus*, p. 146).

[12] εἴ πως : if perhaps, if possible, if in any way.

In the face of other assured utterances by Paul concerning his future expectations (as Rom. 6:5, 8; Rom. 8:38, 39; 1 Cor. 15:51, 52; Phil. 1:23, 3:21, 1 Thess. 4:14,16), these words are not to be considered as expressing any doubt or uncertainty, but rather as an expression of deep

the resurrection from the dead" does not express uncertainty but rather humble expectation and modest self-confidence. Even the apostle—and together with him all who have attained the righteousness of God through faith—must watch and pray continually to abide in the fellowship of Christ's suffering and in conformity to His death, ever dying to himself and to sin and ever crucified with Christ. For only in that way the glorification with Christ, and the perfect knowledge of and sinless communion with the living Lord will be attained by and after the resurrection from the dead. Not until then will the believer experience complete victory after the struggle of faith which is his portion on earth. By speaking of the resurrection "from the dead," Paul does not refer to the general resurrection of all the dead but definitely to the resurrection in glory in which only believers will share,[13] after sharing Christ's sufferings and becoming like Him in His death.

The mystical fellowship and union of the believer with

---

humility and modest self-reliance (cf. also 1 Cor. 9:27). "His apparent uncertainty here of reaching the goal is not distrust in God. It is distrust in himself" (Kennedy, *ad loc.*).

13 $\dot{\varepsilon}\xi\alpha\nu\dot{\alpha}\sigma\tau\alpha\sigma\iota\varsigma$ is a *hapax legomenon* in the N. T. Paul furthermore speaks here of a resurrection $\dot{\varepsilon}\varkappa$ $\nu\varepsilon\varkappa\varrho\tilde{\omega}\nu$ and not $\tau\tilde{\omega}\nu$ $\nu\varepsilon\varkappa\varrho\tilde{\omega}\nu$. '$A\nu\dot{\alpha}\sigma\tau\alpha\sigma\iota\varsigma$ $\tau\tilde{\omega}\nu$ $\nu\varepsilon\varkappa\varrho\tilde{\omega}\nu$ denotes the general resurrection of the dead, but the resurrection *out of the dead*, $\dot{\varepsilon}\varkappa$ $\nu\varepsilon\varkappa\varrho\tilde{\omega}\nu$, always denotes, wherever it is used, the resurrection of the righteous, the resurrection to life and glory, which will not be the case with all the dead. From the context it is clear that Paul here, in speaking of the resurrection, is so completely concentrating upon the righteous and their resurrection to glory, that he does not even mention or in any way reflect upon the unrighteous for the moment. Such is also the case in places like 1 Cor. 15:20—23 and 1 Thess. 4:16, 17.

Christ must consummate finally in the glorified resurrection of the body with and in Christ. To faith this truth is not only a possession of the present but always also still an expectation of the future. It is a matter of certainty but at the same time also an object of hope.

3:12—16

12 Not that I have already obtained, or am already made
perfect: but I press on, if so be that I may lay hold on
that for which also I was laid hold on by Christ Jesus.

13 Brethren, I count not myself yet to have laid hold: but
one thing I do, forgetting the things which are behind,
and stretching forward to the things which are before,

14 I press on toward the goal unto the prize of the high
calling of God in Christ Jesus.

15 Let us therefore, as many as are perfect, be thus minded:
and if in anything ye are otherwise minded, this also shall
God reveal unto you:

16 only, whereunto we have attained, by that same rule let
us walk.

12 The apostle wishes to state clearly to the Church
that, from what was said in the previous verses, the conclusion must not be drawn[1] that he had already reached the
state of perfection in faith and grace after which he was so
fervently longing, since he had given up all for the sake
of Christ. Without mentioning the object in so many words,
he declares that he has not yet obtained or made (it) his
own,[2] and he proceeds: "nor am I already made perfect,"[3]

---

[1] οὐχ ὅτι "not that," is elliptical, and λέγω can readily be understood with it, so that the trend of thought is: "I do not say that,
I do not mean that..." The statement is made by the apostle to
prevent a possible misunderstanding as if he had already attained
perfection.

[2] Codd. D E F G add: ἢ ἤδη δεδικαίωμαι, which is probably an
explanatory insertion of later date.

[3] The perfect τετελείωμαι (in contrast with the preceding Aorist

120

i.e. perfection has not yet been reached, the work of grace
has not yet been carried through to the end, he has not yet
arrived at the stage where what is perfect sets in. By this
perfection he apparently does not mean the glorification
which follows hereafter with the resurrection from the dead
(it is self-evident, indeed, that such an eschatological expectation cannot now already be realised), but the apostle
evidently has in mind the full knowledge of Christ, and the
full-grown communion with Him and conformity to Him
to which he has not yet come, the entire sanctification,
spiritual and moral maturity and perfection which he has
not yet attained.

But he is not going to acquiesce passively in this. "But
I press on to make it my own."⁴ With the utmost exertion

ἔλαβον) denotes a continuous state. Literally translated it is: "(that I
already) have been perfected, made perfect." The verb denotes:
to attain the aim, to carry through to the end, to make perfect or whole.

4   Paul presses on towards it—he has not yet obtained it, he is not
yet perfect, he has not yet "laid hold" (verse 13). This definite and
clear *not yet*, οὐκ ἤδη (12) or οὔπω (13), expressed by someone with
the profound spiritual experience of Paul, is very significant. He is
not yet perfect, has not yet attained it. Hereby is not meant: not yet
wholly perfect, not yet attained *all*, as if a certain measure of perfection
has nonetheless already been attained and certain heights have already
been reached. Just as in the case of entire perfection, so also there is
no partial perfection which the child of God could have at his disposal.
Paul has *not yet*, therefore he yearns for perfection, he presses on to
make it his own, he is eager to grasp it. In himself, by virtue of his
own achievement, he has to confess: *not yet!* It always remains: *not yet*,
but at the same time always also (because Christ had made him His
own): *I press on to grasp it.* The *not yet* does not cause slackening
on the road, but stimulates to perseverance.

This portion of Scripture dismisses: (a) self-righteous perfectionism,
which implies that he has *already* made it his own, has attained it, is

he strives after it, as in a race where one presses on towards the goal (cf. verse 14). Not only to press on, however, but also to overtake, to get hold of, seize, to grasp is his aim. He presses on so that he can apprehend it. This exertion to make it his own arises from the wonderful experience of grace which the apostle himself had by virtue of the fact that Christ had made him His own.[5] His own "apprehending" is the fruit of the fact that Christ had apprehended him, laid hold on him. Here he evidently has in mind his Damascus experience, when Christ laid His hand on him and he came to conversion. Anyone on whom Christ thus lays hold cannot but exert himself to the utmost and press on keenly towards perfection so that he can make it his own (Comp. 2:12, 13—the self-activity of man by virtue of God's own working and influence).

With Paul—as in the case of each believer—the principle holds that he has *not yet made it his own,* and is *not yet perfect.* He is best described as one who is still racing on the course, who is still straining forward to grasp: not with hands already half filled, but still empty, only *viator* and

---

perfect; (b) self-sufficient semi-perfectionism, which is of opinion that he has not yet wholly made it his own, has not yet attained all, and is not yet entirely perfect, but nevertheless has attained *much already,* and to a reasonable extent is already perfect; (c) indolent imperfectionism which is only conscious of the *not yet,* and acquiesces in sinful self-satisfaction, without being urged on to the pursuit of sanctification with all his might.

5   ἐφ' ᾧ indicates the reason why Paul presses on to make it his own, viz. *because* Christ has made him His own. Although the expression can also indicate the purpose here with which Christ made Paul His own, its rendering by *because* is better supported by Paul's use of the expression elsewhere. "The divine grace in Paul's conversion is the moving power in his Christian development" (Vincent).

not yet *comprehensor*. It is still an empty hand, but thereby also an outstretched hand, eager to grasp. "The Christian life is more one of taking than of having, more one of becoming pious than of being pious" (Luther). This urge towards sanctification and the striving after perfection is unavoidable for anyone of whom Christ has laid hold with the divine purpose that he should be holy and blameless (cf. Eph. 1:4). A God-given imperative—*I must!*—is active in him, and a God-given resolution—*I will!*—incites and urges him on on the road to holiness. He must accept the *not yet* as the actual state, and yet he cannot acquiesce in it, and must press on towards perfection, because God wills it, and because it is his destination.

13-14 The same idea which is expressed in verse 12, is accentuated again in verses 13, 14. In contrast with others who possibly hold such a self-sufficient view of themselves that they have already made it their own and are already perfect, or who may suppose that the beloved and devoted apostle has surely attained it, Paul declares[6] very emphatically that he considers[7] that he himself has *not yet* made it his own. Not apprehended, not yet attained, still imperfect! That is the present state and condition.

But—no acquiescence in this! "One thing" is of supreme importance, and that one thing he does: he forgets "the things which are behind." Not that he does not remember

---

6 The translation: "I consider that I myself have not yet made it my own" is preferable to: "I do not consider that I (myself) have made it my own." The reading οὔπω (thus Aleph A D) is better suited to the trend of thought in verse 14 as well as to the οὐκ ἤδη of verse 12, than the reading οὐ (of B F G).

7 λογίζομαι expresses the idea of considering, reasoning, reckoning, judging. Cf. Kittel IV, pp. 291 f.

them, and does not know of them any more, but his mind is not fixed on them any longer. He does not look back on them in such a way that they impede his further progress. The recollections of what he was in his former unconverted state must not paralyse and discourage him; disappointments and temptations of the past must not depress him; the thought of what God had already done for him and through him must not lead him to slackness and self-satisfaction. The hand is put to the plough and he will not look back.

On the contrary, he "strains forward to what lies ahead." The verb used here is very descriptive, and calls to mind the attitude of a runner on the course, who with body bent forward, hand stretched to the fore, and eye fixed on the goal, strains forward with the utmost exertion in pursuit of his purpose. So the apostle presses on toward the goal[8] on which he fixes his eye in the race of faith to attain the prize of the perfect fellowship with Christ, and his glorification with Christ in the immaculate heritage of heaven hereafter (cf. 2 Tim. 4:8; Rev. 2:10). This prize is connected with the upward (heavenly, heavenward) call of God which he received at his conversion, when God's saving call to everlasting life came to him "in Christ Jesus," i.e. by His merit and in communion with Him. Paul is apprehended by Christ (verse 12), is called by God in Christ (verse 14), and the prize of this calling towards which he presses forward with all his might, is the everlasting, heavenly

---

8 σκοπός (derived from σκοπέω) indicates that on which I fix my gaze, at which I am looking, i.e. the aim, the goal. Hence also the pressing on takes place κατὰ σκοπὸν, according to the mark on which I fix my look.

glory. "Paul knows that with this possession he is rich in his boundless poverty" (Barth).

15-16 Where Paul now speaks of himself and others who are perfect (in RSV translated "mature")[9]—after his emphatic statement in verse 12 that he is not yet perfect—he probably uses the word *teleios* (perfect) here, not in the sense of ethical perfection, but of perfection in principle. We have an analogy in Paul's use of the word *hagios* (holy) in connection with saints. Their subjective state or condition as believers can in no way be termed holy or irreproachable in an ethical sense, but nevertheless believers or saints are indeed separated unto God and consecrated to Him, and therefore in principle may be considered as holy in Christ.

Perfection fundamentally and in principle consists in "the true connection with Christ, the true faith in Him, the true

---

9 τέλειος translated by "mature" in RSV but really meaning "perfect," can evidently not be taken here as having the same meaning as τετελείωμαι in verse 12. There something is indicated which Paul has not yet attained, he is not yet perfect; here, however, he and other believers, are called perfect or mature. Vincent wishes to distinguish (with regard to τέλειος) between absolute perfection (whereby no further striving is possible or necessary), and relative perfection, in the sense of full-grown, mature, in contrast with former infirmities and ignorance. With the latter "perfection" there is still room for growth and for a higher endeavour and a straining towards the goal. Barth is of the opinion that the Christian perfection of which Paul speaks, taken paradoxically, consists in the Christian imperfection, in the striving toward the goal. It seems, however, that we have just to differentiate here between the principial perfection which all believers in Christ possess, and the ethical perfection towards which all must constantly strive, and of which no one can boast that he has already attained it.

knowledge of Him" (Greijdanus), and this Paul possessed—and so do all true believers,—although it is not yet to such an extent and in such fulness as they actually desire it. Just as a little child is a perfect human being, but still is far from perfect in his development as man, so the true child of God is also perfect in all parts, although not yet perfect in all the stages of his development in faith. In verse 12 Paul confessed that he was not yet perfect in all the stages, but here he confesses his perfection in all parts, as child of God.

"Let therefore, as many as are perfect, be thus minded." Herewith he refers to verse 13, to the forgetting of what lies behind and to the straining forward to what lies ahead, in humble confession that we are not there yet, but at the same time with a keen and active desire and striving thereafter. Whoever is "perfect" or "mature" must not be characterised by indolent self-satisfaction, but by definite and purposeful upward endeavour.

"And if in any thing ye are otherwise minded," if members of the church at Philippi do not see the matter in this light, think otherwise and accentuate differently, and do not feel the urge to sanctification as strongly as Paul does,[10] then God will reveal that[11] also to them; God will

---

[10] "It was entirely possible that many of his readers, although having a genuine faith in Christ, and fully accepting the doctrine of justification by faith, might not have apprehended his profound views of mystical union, or have had the same clear ideas as himself concerning certain practical applications of doctrine; even that they might not have felt the impulse to higher spiritual attainment in its full stringency, and might have been inclined to regard his conduct and sentiments in certain particulars as exaggerated. Such facts are familiar to every Christian pastor" (Vincent).

[11] Bengel relates this τοῦτο to the first τοῦτο of the sentence, which then means: God will reveal *this* also to you, viz. that which Paul

make the matter clear to them, and by the teaching of His Word and Spirit will guide His people into all the truth (cf. John 16:13).

"Only, whereunto we have attained, by that same rule let us walk" (literally: walk in line with[12]). Notwithstanding all difference or divergence of opinion which there may by, there must be progress on the royal road of the revealed truth. God may give further revelations, but the present duty is to walk in the light of that unto which the believers have already come. We have to move forward in the same line, one of mind, true to what we have already attained.[13]

---

impressed upon you and which you must consider, that, although you have not attained it, you should continually strive after perfection with all your might.

In a related sense Calvin too interprets this clause: God will reveal to them what they do not yet know, and will show them that Paul is right in what he said.

[12] The verb στοιχεῖν (comp. στοῖχος = line or row), means: to stand in a row, or walk in a line, i.e. walk in the same line. The imperative infinitive, to express a general injunction, is used here, as elsewhere with Paul, cf. Rom. 12:15.

[13] In contrast with this short reading of Aleph A B, the TR, with K L P, after στοιχεῖν adds: κανόνι, τὸ αὐτὸ φρονεῖν.

It is difficult to give a fluent translation of this compressed sentence. Its meaning is best rendered by: "Only (nevertheless), whereto we have already come, walk according to it (walk in line with it)." Lightfoot paraphrases it as follows: "Our footsteps must not swerve from the line in which we have hitherto trodden." Comm. p. 152.

3:17—19

> 17 Brethren, be ye imitators together of me, and mark them that so walk even as ye have us for an ensample.
>
> 18 For many walk, of whom I told you often, and now tell you even weeping, that they are the enemies of the cross of Christ;
>
> 19 whose end is perdition, whose god is the belly, and whose glory is in their shame, who mind earthly things.

17 As elsewhere in this chapter (verses 1 and 13) the apostle addresses himself to the "brethren"—an expression by which he denotes his intimate spiritual attachment to the believers there as well as his unity and equality with them—and appeals to them all, "one and all," to become his followers.[1] Only that person in whose life the grace of Christ is seen, can ask others to be as he himself is (cf. 1 Cor. 11:1). Not only Paul, but also other servants of the gospel who were like-minded, are held up as examples. "Mark those who live as you have an example in *us*." Herewith the apostle evidently includes the fellow sender of the Letter, Timothy, and probably also Epaphroditus (cf. 2:25,29). Paul's own example, of which he desires imitation, is depicted

---

[1] Here we have an unusual combination of μιμηταί with συν. It does not mean: "Be followers *together with me* (of Christ)," but "Be together followers *of me*," fellow-followers of me, co-imitators of me.

The confidence (and responsibility) to call others to follow us or to draw the attention of others on our example, can only be there if we ourselves have become followers of Christ, as 1 Cor. 11:1 puts so clearly. In us—without Christ—there is nothing good to imitate; only what is in us of Christ is worth imitating.

from verse 7 onward, as follows: What was gain is counted as loss for the sake of Christ (7); the loss of all things was suffered in order to gain Christ (8); the aim is directed not on his own righteousness, but on that which is from God through faith (9); perfection is not yet attained, but is eagerly pursued (12), and what lies behind is forgotten so that with all his might he could press toward the goal for the prize of the upward call of God in Christ (14). Such is the life and walk of Paul and his fellow-workers. Something of Christ and the work of His grace and of the power of His resurrection and the fellowship with His sufferings can be seen in them. Therefore their example can call forth imitation by other believers (cf. 1 Cor. 15:10, 1 Tim. 1:16).

18-19 All do not live and walk in this way. There are those of whom the apostle has repeatedly said during the ten years since the foundation of the church by him (Acts 16), and on visits to them afterwards (Acts 20:1—3, 6), —and he repeats it now with tears and with deep emotion—that they are enemies[2] of the cause of Christ, although they move in Christian circles. It is a state of affairs which causes tears, that there are many who are "enemies of the cross of Christ." It is not enmity directed against the cross as the tree on which Jesus hung, but against that for which the cross stands, the ideology of Christianity. Enmity against the cross may mean any anti-Christian action, any opposition to the gospel of which the preaching

---

2 The original here is not that many *live* as enemies (which would be ὡς ἐχθροι), but that there are many "of whom I *told* you that they are enemies of the cross of Christ." Literal translation therefore: "For many live, of whom I have often told you and now tell you even with tears, that they are the enemies of the cross of Christ."

of the cross is the pivot and centre; or it may also be the opposition of self-sufficiency against the demands made by the gospel of the cross with regard to the taking up of the cross personally and sharing the suffering of Christ. But here it can best be understood of the Judaistic opposition to the gospel of the cross, which is the gospel of free grace as preached by Paul. Paul had already on several occasions warned against those who confessed Christ but took offence at the cross, and demanded the keeping of the law as necessary for salvation. The cross of Christ and the all-sufficient merits of His death on the cross and of His concilatory work, were being denied. Man's *own* righteousness, by keeping Law and circumcision, was an enemy of the righteousness which is through the cross of Christ. Paul had already described the Judaizers as "dogs, evil-workers, concision" (verse 2), and here he calls them "the enemies (not only enemies, but *the* enemies) of the cross of Christ."[3] Elsewhere Paul says of them that they "are severed from Christ and have fallen away from grace" (Gal. 5:4; cf. verses 1—4 and also 6:12, 13). The enmity against the cross here therefore reveals itself in the spiritual pride which puts its trust in its own righteousness, and will not live by faith alone and expect salvation only from the merits of the cross of Christ.

The enemies of the cross are now more closely described in a four fold way. (1) *Their end is perdition:* spiritual and moral as well as physical ruin is the end to which their actions are leading. (2) *Their god is the belly:* although such a description could suit sensualists, people of dissolute

---

[3] The definite article τοὺς before ἔχθρους does not only describe them as enemies, but definitely as *the* enemies.

character, Paul in Rom. 16:18 designates people like the Judaists, who sow dissension in the churches and are the cause of offence against the doctrine, as people "who serve their own belly." While the New Testament nowhere describes licentiousness as "serving the belly," the Judaists were the people who enforced the observance of all kinds of laws relating to meat and drink, by which they did not do justice to the all-sufficient merits of the cross of Christ. "Touch not and taste not—eat and eat not" became religion to them. (For this element in the heresy at Colossae, cf. Col. 2:20—23). (3) *Their glory is in their shame:* with sensualists this would mean addiction to humiliating lusts which serve to their disgrace and shame. But in the case of the Judaists the word *shame* here can be taken as meaning *nakedness* (or the private parts), by which accordingly is meant that they glory in the circumcised part of their body.[4] They boast of their circumcision, they associate their glory with their circumcised flesh, ignoring the spiritual bearing which it has on Christ and His cross. Of the Judaists Paul elsewhere said in this connection: "They desire to have you circumcised that they may *glory in your flesh*" (Gal. 6:13). (4) *They mind earthly things:* by this not necessarily carnal sins are meant, but the direction of their thoughts towards earthly things, worldly-mindedness, a life ordered according to worldly measures. The Judaistic piety makes a god of the belly, finds glory in its circumcised body, and is there-

---

4 αἰσχύνη can here have the meaning of shame (as part of the body), as is the case sometimes in the LXX (Nah. 3:5). Barth takes both consecutive phrases here as having the same meaning and puts it thus: "Their god is their belly and their glory is in their shame! is once again an allusion to their circumcision, which in concreteness of presentation leaves nothing to be desired."

for nothing else but earthly-mindedness, destined for destruction and ruin, and—in by-passing the cross of Christ and turning the back on the righteousness which is from God through faith—is nothing else but base enmity against the cross of Christ (cf. Gal. 6:12—15; 5:2—4).

3:20, 21

20 For our citizenship is in heaven; whence also we wait for a Saviour, the Lord Jesus Christ:

21 who shall fashion anew the body of our humiliation, that it may be conformed to the body of his glory, according to the working whereby he is able even to subject all things unto himself.

20 Over against the earthly-mindedness of the Judaist Paul now mentions the heavenly citizenship of the Christian believer, and his expectation for the future. It is a twofold contrast[1] which is made: viz. *we* and *they, heavenly* and *earthly.* "Our citizenship, or commonwealth (with full accent on *our,* according to the position of the word) is in heaven." Not the earth but heaven is the fatherland of the Christian, the state or kingdom to which he belongs and where he enjoys rights and privileges. His conduct of life will therefore in agreement therewith not be earthly minded but heavenly minded. An expectation of the parousia is furthermore associated with heaven, for thence[2] the Lord Jesus Christ is expected[3] as Saviour and Redeemer. His

---

[1] The causal word $\gamma \grave{\alpha} \varrho$ links up with the preceding reference to *them* who set *their* minds on earthly things, things irreconcilable with *our* high calling and contrary to *our* manner of life, for *our* commonwealth is in heaven.

[2] $\grave{\varepsilon} \xi$ $o\grave{\vartheta}$ is used adverbially, and refers to $o\grave{\upsilon}\varrho\alpha\nu o\tilde{\iota}\varsigma$ which, although plural in form, is singular in meaning.

[3] $\grave{\alpha}\pi\varepsilon\varkappa\delta\varepsilon\chi\acute{o}\mu\varepsilon\theta\alpha$ denotes eager and longing expectation. The verb is generally used in connection with the second coming of Christ, i.e. in an eschatological sense. Cf. Kittel, TWNT, II, 55.

advent will complete the salvation of redeemed mankind and bring with it full deliverance from all remaining sins and infirmities, and the perfection of the salvation which is already initially experienced here. The whole creation is waiting for deliverance from the bondage to corruption (Rom. 8:21), and redeemed man for the ultimate redemption of the body (Rom. 8:23).

21 With the coming of Christ the transformation of our weak and corruptible bodies to the likeness of His glorious body will take place. Literally the original reads: "the body of our lowliness," i.e. the body connected with our present mortal existence, carnal, broken by sin, subjected to infirmities and suffering and decay. The change which the body will undergo will not only be an external one, but will affect the whole form and mode of existence. It will become like unto Christ's "glorious body" or literally: "the body of His glory," the spiritual, heavenly, glorified body with which He is invested after His exaltation. This glorification is described more elaborately in 1 Cor. 15:42—44, 49, in so far as the dead are concerned, and in 1 Cor. 15:51—54, in so far as those still in life at the advent of Christ are concerned.

Such a change in form of the believers is nothing less than a miracle of Christ's omnipotence. It takes place by the power "whereby he is able even to subject all things unto himself." The divine power[4] is always a power at work, an active divine energy which in addition to everything else which He can, is also able to subject all things to Himself. His is

---

4 ἐνέργεια, power, energy, (divine) working, is a word only found with Paul, and which is always used to denote divine or supernatural power. Cf. Col. 1:29; 2:12. Also Kittel, TWNT, II, 649.

a sovereign power to which all things are subordinate—all earthly power and authority, enemies and death (cf. 1 Cor. 15:24–27; Eph. 1:21, 22). This power of Christ is the guarantee that He is able to make our body of lowliness like unto His body of glory. And this is the future expectation of those whose citizenship is in heaven, and who look forward to the coming of their Lord with longing and in readiness.

For the church of Christ continually lives between remembrance and expectation.

CHAPTER IV

EXHORTATION TO STEADFASTNESS AND UNANIMITY

4:1—3

1 Wherefore, my brethren beloved and longed for, my joy and crown, so stand fast in the Lord, my beloved.

2 I exhort Euodia, and I exhort Syntyche, to be of the same mind in the Lord.

3 Yea, I beseech thee also, true yokefellow, help these women, for they labored with me in the gospel, with Clement also, and the rest of my fellow-workers, whose names are in the book of life.

1 The call to steadfastness—previously also made (1:27) —is very closely allied here to the preceding verses 18—21 by the connecting word "wherefore".[1] Therefore—because there are many enemies of the cross, and also because the believers are looking forward to the coming of their Lord and Saviour which will involve their own glorification, the church is exhorted to stand firm.

The church is addressed as "my beloved brethren," a much more intimate address than the "brethren" of 3:1 and 3:17, and to this several other expressions are now added whereby the apostle gives utterance to his affection for them and his attachment to them. The brethren are not only *beloved* but are fervently *longed for* by a heart which goes out towards them, who are the *joy and crown* of the apostle (cf. a similar expression in 1 Thess. 2:19). The church gives

---

[1] This verse—introduced by ὥστε —forms a fit conclusion to the preceding chapter, and could easily be grouped with the last verses (3:18—21).

him cause for great rejoicing in that they accepted and lived according to the gospel which was preached to them, and for this reason it is the crown[2] or garland of victory for the apostle who founded the church, an evidence of the fruits of his labour, the proof that "he did not run in vain or labour in vain" (2:16), and the reward for his faithful service and devotion. An appeal is made to them, whom he addresses as "beloved" for a second time, "thus to stand fast" (as he had admonished them), "in the Lord," i.e. in His fellowship and in attachment to Him and His cause.

2-3 Special admonitions are now directed to individual persons in the church. Two women in the church, Euodia and Syntyche, are especially entreated "to be of the same mind," or to agree (a matter to which the whole church on various occasions had already been exhorted, 1:27, 2:2). Who they were[3] and what the nature of their differences were, is not stated. They were (as appears from verse 3) women who had laboured side by side with the apostle in the gospel: spiritual workers in the church, believing and influential women. Therefore it was all the more reason why there had

---

[2] A king's crown is usually denoted by $\delta\iota\acute{a}\delta\eta\mu a$, while $\sigma\tau\acute{\epsilon}\varphi a\nu o\varsigma$ indicates the crown of a conqueror, the laurel of victory or a festive garland.

[3] The allegorical explanation by F. C. Baur and the Tübingen School that the two names stand for the Jewish Christian section and the gentile Christian section of the church at Philippi, is definitely to be dismissed as the result of their preconceived and unproved conception of an "Unionstendenz" in the Pauline Letters with regard to the two tendencies in the early Christian Church.

Similarly the view that we have to do here with the names of a married couple (e.g. the gaoler of Philippi and his wife), is not convincing, and is definitely contradicted by the reference to the two names by $a\mathring{v}\tau a\tilde{\iota}\varsigma$ in verse 3.

to be no discord or quarrel between them, but on the contrary, harmony and unanimity in the Lord, in attachment to Him and in His service, was essential.

In addition to this admonition, Syzygus is also[4] requested to assist them in acquiring the desired harmony. Syzygus[5] is to be taken here as the proper name of a person who—just as in the case of the two women and Clement—for the rest is entirely unknown to us. The primary meaning of the name is *yokefellow* or *companion,* and if the word is here intended as an ordinary generic name—as many versions of Scripture take it—then the unnamed "yokefellow" must have stood in a particular relation to Paul and his work, by being indicated by such a designation without further

---

[4] The reading καὶ is very weakly supported in contrast with ναὶ (a *yes* accentuated) by Aleph A B D E F G K L P.

[5] The question here is whether the proper name Σύζυγος is meant or the common name σύζυγος. In the immediate context we prefer the former. A person's name at Philippi is mentioned, probably one of the bishops to whom the Letter is definitely addressed (1:1). The fact that Σύζυγος has not yet been discovered on inscriptions as a proper name, need not prevent our assumption that such a name really existed.

All kinds of conjectures have been made to fix the identity of the person, on the supposition that no proper name is intended here, but "yokefellow" or "companion" in general. This varies from Timothy and Silas, fellow founders with Paul of the church, and Epaphroditus, the carrier of the Letter (so Lightfoot), to Paul's wife (Clem. Alex., Erasmus), the husband of one of the women Euodia or Syntyche (Chrysostomus), Lydia (Renan), and even Christ (Wieseler), which is, however, very far fetched.

The accompanying adjective γνήσιε, going with a proper name Σύζυγε, could be understood in the sense of genuine, true to his name, rightly so called, really. Cf. Str.-B. III, 623. Goodwin, *Harmony and Comm. on the Life of St. Paul,* p. 68.

comment. But then the difficulty still remains as to what person, what fellow worker and yokefellow of Paul, was meant thereby, and why he was so directly addressed in a letter directed to the *church,* without being called by his real name.

The qualification "true" or "genuine" before Syzygus, probably implies that Syzygus is truly so called, that he really is what his name denotes, that he is a true yokefellow, a *syzygus* in truth, that his name is a true reflection of his character.

Concerning the women whom Syzygus has to help, Paul states that they[6] "laboured side by side with me in the gospel," that when the church was founded or on later occasions, they exerted themselves and eagerly co-operated in the interests of the gospel with the apostle, and also with Clement[7] and the other fellow labourers whom Paul had at Philippi "whose names are in the book[8] of life." Although Paul does not call them by name, or their names are already forgotten on earth because they died in the meantime, yet their names are known to God and are entered in His book of life (cf. Rev. 3:5, 20:12, also Luke 10:20). God knows them, although the world does not know them, and they are assured of life everlasting as a gift of God's grace; and for this reason "their names have a glory greater than that of historical renown" (Kennedy).

---

[6] *αἵτινες* instead of *αἱ* indicates the nature of the women as distinguished from others: "as those who" instead of only "who".

[7] Clement is for the rest unknown to us. That he was Clement, the later bishop of Rome, rests only on agreement in name, but has no historical support.

[8] The idea of a book in which the names are entered—apart from such instances as Luke 10:20, Rev. 3:5, 13:8, 20:12 in the N. T. is found frequently in the O. T. Cf. Exod. 32:32, Dan. 12:1.

4 Rejoice in the Lord always: again I will say, Rejoice.

5 Let your forbearance be known unto all men. The Lord is at hand.

6 In nothing be anxious; but in everything by prayer and supplication with thanksgiving let your requests be made known unto God.

7 And the peace of God, which passeth all understanding, shall guard your hearts and your thoughts in Christ Jesus.

8 Finally, brethren, whatsoever things are true, whatsoever things are honorable, whatsoever things are just, whatsoever things are pure, whatsoever things are lovely, whatsoever things are of good report; if there be any virtue, and if there be any praise, think on these things.

9 The things which ye both learned and received and heard and saw in me, these things do: and the God of peace shall be with you.

4 Rejoice everywhere and under all circumstances! Here the keynote of the Letter is sounded once again (cf. 1:4, 1:18, 2:17, 18, 3:1), and it comes to the believer as a divine imperative. "To rejoice, to comfort himself, to strengthen himself, to be cheered, is—as understood by Christians—a command just as any other" (Barth). Not circumstances decide whether there will be joy, but *in the Lord,* in living fellowship with Him, the believer can and must rejoice under all circumstances. Hence the apostle's repetition of the exhortation: "Rejoice!"

5 Next to joy, forbearance,[1] or rather: goodwill, fair-

---

[1] τὸ ἐπιεικές as neut. adj. with the article, has the same meaning as the noun ἐπιείκεια, which denotes reasonableness, goodwill, modera-

ness, magnanimity. This must become known to all men, must be seen by all in everyday life and deeds. "The Lord is at hand" can be understood in spatial and local sense, that the Lord is near to us and that His eyes rest on all our doings as an encouragement to do His will; but more likely the preceding exhortations must be seen in the light of the truth that the advent of the Lord[2] is at hand, and that therefore the church is exhorted to joy and reasonableness and forbearance towards fellowmen. (Cf. the same trend of thought in James 5:8—"Be ye also patient; establish your hearts, for the coming of the Lord is at hand").

6 No anxiety! There must be no anxiety or worry about anything (cf. Matt. 6:25—34). To care is a virtue, but to foster cares is sin, for such anxiety is not trust in God, but a trusting in oneself, which comes to inward suffering, fears and worry. The cure for anxiety is prayer to God and commitment of our way unto the Lord. "In everything by prayer[3] and supplication (adoration and entreaty) with thanksgiving let your requests be made known to God." Requests born of material or spiritual need, must be brought to God. We must, however, not only petition and entreat, but also thank for blessings already received, for infallible promises by God, and for the loving care of the Father, who

---

tion, magnanimity, friendliness, forbearance, and which is the opposite of: strictly claiming your rights, seeking yourself, and not being obliging towards others. Cf. Kittel II, 585.

[2] From this we need not infer that Paul expected an immediate coming of Christ. Cf. his assertions in his Letters written earlier, 1 Thess. 5:24, 2 Thess. 2:1—3.

[3] προσευχή is commonly used for prayer in general as invocation of God, while δέησις denotes entreaty or supplication, the prayer of want and need.

provided in the past and will also provide in the future, and to whom we may leave our way with confidence (cf. 1 Pet. 5:7). Not to care yourself, but to let God care: so through our thanksgiving all honour is given to God. No prayer, no supplication without thanksgiving!

7 A further blessing awaits those who thus take all their cares to the Lord in prayer. The peace of God will keep their hearts and minds in Christ Jesus. Of this peace which God gives, the peace of mind which God works, it is furthermore said that it "passes all understanding." This can be taken as meaning in general that no human mind can grasp or fathom or comprehend the greatness and fulness and the glory of the peace which God gives (cf. Eph. 3:19: "To know the love of Christ which passeth knowledge"). In close connection with verse 6, however, it probably means that the peace which God gives excels and surpasses all our own intellectual calculations[4] and considerations, all our contemplations and premeditated ideas of how to get rid of our cares—and which after all *cannot* completely remove our faint-heartedness and worry, and restore peace and calm to our minds. What God gives, surpasses all that we ask or think (cf. Eph. 3:20).

The peace of God will keep watch over and guard hearts and minds[5]—the world of affection and thought—against

---

[4]   νοῦς is the thinking intellect and mind, which perceives, turns the matter over, considers and plans.

[5]   φρουρεῖν is better translated here in the forceful meaning of: *to keep guard* than merely as "keep" (RSV). "God's peace shall stand sentry, shall keep guard over your hearts" (Lightfoot). "The peace of God is the garrison of the soul in all the experiences of its life, defending it from the external assaults of temptation and anxiety, and disciplining all lawless desires and imaginations within..." (Kennedy).

worries and temptations towards anxiety; will keep watch over heart and mind so that nothing can cause unrest and discord, because everything is placed trustingly in the hands of God by the prayer of faith. This, however, takes place only *in Christ Jesus,* in our attachment to Him and fellowship with Him. Apart from Him there is no surety or guarantee for peace of mind, but whosoever is in Christ, is entrusted to the infallible safe-keeping of the peace of God.

8 In the exhortation to Christian virtuousness several matters are furthermore brought forward to be considered, to be weighed and taken into account in Christian life. Amongst these are mentioned: whatever (as many things as) is true, honourable (worthy), just (in the right relation to God and man), pure (in a moral sense), lovely (attractive and amiable) and gracious (praiseworthy); and next to these, without further comment: any virtue (moral excellence) and any praise[6] (thing approved and therefore worthy of praise).

9 These things must, however, not only be contemplated, but also be carried into effect. With this in view the apostle now refers to his own instruction and example. "The things which ye both learned and received" refers to what they received by way of instruction and what they accepted and appropriated for themselves; "what you heard and saw in me[7]" points to Paul's preaching to them at Philippi and his virtuous way of life which they could observe. All that

---

6 Codd. D E F G add ἐπιστήμης after ἔπαινος, which would mean: praise of knowledge, praiseworthy knowledge.

7 Although ἐν ἐμοί, according to the construction of the sentence, only goes with the last verb, the meaning undoubtedly applies to all four of the verbs, for in all things Paul was to them the spiritual teacher and example.

they had received from Paul by way of teaching and admonition, and by what they heard from his mouth and saw in his Christian example, this they had to do, they had to act accordingly.

For all who act thus, who combine Christian doctrine and practice in daily life in such a way, a gracious promise is made: The God of peace will be with them. Not only the peace of God (verse 7) will be their share, but the God of peace Himself, who is the source of all spiritual blessings, will favour them with His peace and be with them always.

CONTENT IN ALL CIRCUMSTANCES

10 But I rejoice in the Lord greatly, that now at length ye have revived your thought for me; wherein ye did indeed take thought, but ye lacked opportunity.

11 Not that I speak in respect of want: for I have learned, in whatsoever state I am, therein to be content.

12 I know how to be abased, and I know also how to abound: in everything and in all things have I learned the secret both to be filled and to be hungry, both to abound and to be in want.

13 I can do all things in him that strengtheneth me.

In this pericope Paul not only expresses his joy with regard to the Church's real and tangible interest in him, but also bears witness to the fact that he has already learned the secret of being content and satisfied with his lot, whether he prospered or not, because under all the changing circumstances of life he is strengthened by the sustaining power of Christ.

10 The arrival of Epaphroditus with gifts for him from Philippi (4:18; cf. 2:25, 30), was the cause of great joy[1] to Paul—not only natural joy for the gift received, but a joy experienced in the Lord, because the gift stood in connection with the cause of the Lord, was sent as a support for His servant in prison, and gave evidence of Christian love and sympathy in the Church. It was a proof that the Church at last again (or once more) thought of Paul's interests, and

---

1 ἐχάρην can either be taken as aor. ingress., denoting the beginning of his joy at the arrival of Epaphroditus, or as epistolary aor., past in form but present in meaning.

revived[2] their concern for him. Immediately, however, the apostle admits that they were indeed mindful of his interests, of help and care for him, but did not have a suitable opportunity or time.[3] It was therefore not a lack of concern or of willingness to help, but the suitable occasion to do something for him or to send him something had been lacking. The circumstances for it had not been favourable to them.

11 The reference to his joy on account of their renewed interest and help, was, however, not due to the fact that at present he suffered want or was in need; for under all circumstances—also that of want or privation—he had learned to be content,[4] to be satisfied with what he was and had, to be inwardly independent of the varying outward circumstances.

12 He *has learned* (verse 11) in the school of life, and now he *knows* by virtue of his own experience both how to be abased by need and want and adverse circumstances, and how to be provided for in an abundant way. "In everything and in all things" (in every respect‧and in all matters) he has been taught and initiated.[5] Such circumstances of life are not strange to him; he knows what they are, and by his own experience he has learned their secrets: both to have

---

[2] ἀνεθάλετε can also be taken in an intransitive sense: "You have revived with regard to your concern for me."

[3] ἠκαιρεῖσθε from ἀκαιρεῖν: to have no *kairos*, opportunity, suitable time (*hapax leg.* in the N. T.).

[4] Beatus est praesentibus, qualiacunque sunt, contentus (Seneca).

[5] μεμύημαι from μυεῖσθαι, a word used in connection with the rites of the mystery religions. Meaning: to be initiated, to learn the secrets.

plenty[6] and to hunger, both to have abundance and to suffer want.

Plenty and hunger, abundance and want—in all these Paul has been initiated. He knows the joys and the cares of life, prosperity and adversity, "good" days and "evil" days, favourable and unfavourable circumstances. And he has learned to be content under all circumstances, be they good or be they evil.

13 The confession which at the same time reveals the secret of his contentment under all circumstances, does not stay out. "I can do all things in (or through) Him[7] (Christ) that strengtheneth me." He sees his way—and has the strength—to meet any circumstance of life which may arise, through the gracious help of his Lord. There is no dependence on his own strength or ability, but a reliance on the Lord, and a trust in the sustaining Christ who gives him strength. He who is weak in himself, is strong in Christ and in His power (cf. 2 Cor. 12:10). Paul can face all circumstances of life as they come, and be strong, only in the strength which Christ Himself in His great mercy grants him, and which is experienced in intimate fellowship with Christ.

---

[6] χορτάζειν really means: to feed, originally used of animals. Meaning: to have plenty, to be satisfied or full.

[7] The reading χριστῷ at the end of the sentence is found with E F G K L P, but is wanting in Aleph A B D. It is probably a later addition for the sake of clarity (comp. 1 Tim. 1:12; 2 Cor. 12:9).

14 Howbeit ye did well that ye had fellowship with my affliction.

15 And ye yourselves also know, ye Philippians, that in the beginning of the gospel, when I departed from Macedonia, no church had fellowship with me in the matter of giving and receiving but ye only;

16 for even in Thessalonica ye sent once and again unto my need.

17 Not that I seek for the gift; but I seek for the fruit that increaseth to your account.

18 But I have all things, and abound: I am filled, having received from Epaphroditus the things that came from you, an odor of a sweet smell, a sacrifice acceptable, well-pleasing to God.

14 Paul does not wish to create the impression that the gift was not welcome or necessary, because he alleged that he was content under all circumstances. What they did was being appreciated: they did well by acting in this manner. They thereby shared with him in his tribulation. They helped him to carry his burden by means of their material gift, their fellow-feeling and intercession, their interest and their willingness to make sacrifices, and so they had a share in alleviating his hardship in captivity. Their partnership in the gospel (1:5) led to a fellowship in his suffering for the sake of Christ.

15-16 The gift brought to the apostle by Epaphroditus (cf. verses 10, 14, 18) was not the first nor the only token of assistance rendered to him. "In the beginning of the gospel",[1] when the gospel was preached for the first time in those parts, viz. Macedonia and Greece, the Philippians already granted him financial aid and supported his work. When he departed from Macedonia (in which Philippi and Thessalonica were situated) to Achaia (Athens and Corinth), no other church contributed towards his income or towards defraying his expenses[2] except Philippi only (cf. 2 Cor. 11:8, 9). For the rest Paul, in addition to his work as a preacher, earned his living through his own manual labour (cf. 1 Thess. 2:9, 2 Thess. 3:8, 1 Cor. 4:12).

The support to the apostle, however, did not only start after his departure from Macedonia, but even while he was there, for[3] in Thessalonica which Paul visited immediately after Philippi, they once and again[4] sent him substantial support towards alleviating his need.

17 Paul does not wish to be misunderstood,[5] because of what he stated in verses 15 and 16, as if he desired their

---

[1] The second missionary journey of Paul, during which the church of Philippi was established, was "the beginning of the gospel" in those parts (Europe), although the gospel had already been preached earlier in other regions. Between the first preaching at Philippi and the writing of this Letter from Rome, a period of more than ten years elapsed.

[2] $εἰς \ λόγον \ δόσεως \ καὶ \ λήμψεως$ is a business term, and denotes the account of expenditure and receipts, of giving and taking.

[3] If we translate $ὅτι$ with *that*, we make this verse co-ordinate with the previous one, and $ὅτι$ (just as in verse 15) dependent on $οἴδατε$ (so Weiss, Kennedy), which, however, is unlikely.

[4] Literally: both once and twice; therefore: several times, more than once. Cf. for the same expression 1 Thess. 2:18.

[5] $οὐχ \ ὅ$ cf. verse 11 for the same expression. There he dismisses the idea that it was owing to his needs that he rejoiced at their gift to him; here he dismisses the idea that he was anxious to have the gift for its own sake and for the advantage it would bring to him.

gifts as such on account of the advantage which he gained thereby. On the contrary, he does not seek the material gift, but the spiritual fruit, revealing itself in the gift. The fruit he is seeking is not so much the fruit resting on his preaching of the gospel to them (thus Greijdanus), or the fruit consisting in any further labour made possible to him (thus Barth), but is the spiritual fruit which their deed of generosity yields unto themselves, the retroactive blessing resting on those who accomplish the deed of love.[6] It is the fruit "which increases to your credit," for the offering of the gift enriches the giver spiritually and is entered on his account in his favour, to his credit. There is a "recompense which is placed on your account and increases with each fresh demonstration of your love" (Lightfoot). More than the advantage which a gift yields to him personally, Paul desires the fruit of spiritual enrichment among them,[7] an increase in that disposition which is born of Christian love and leads to deeds of charity in the Name of the Lord, and which gives clear evidence of grace received.

18 Paul received in full, and nothing more is owing to him.[8] He received all things which their love could do for

---

[6] "The liberal soul shall be made fat, and he that watereth shall be watered also himself" (Prov. 11:25). "Every act of Christian ministry develops and enriches him who performs it" (Vincent); it brings a "Segenslohn der ihnen aus ihrem Geben und Opfern erwächst" (Str.-B. III, 624).

[7] "The apostle lauds their generosity, because he wished to increase their devotion by his praise, and because he expected more fruit from them which would be put on their account with God" (Zanchius).

[8] ἀπέχω is a word generally used in connection with a receipt or settlement of payment. The obligation has been honoured, the debt has been settled, and therefore: I have received.

him and what he needed in his peculiar circumstances, and
that in abundance. Since he received their gifts brought to
him by Epaphroditus, he is filled and his want is changed
into fulness. The gifts they sent[9] are a lovely fragrance and
a pleasant acceptable offering which is pleasing to God (cf.
Hebr. 13:16). It is a fragrant incense-offering most pleasing
to God. The gift to Paul obtains a greater worth and a
higher significance when seen as an offering brought to God.
What was given towards Paul's needs was sacrificed to God
Himself. For, indeed, what is done to one of the least of His
brethren, is done to the Lord Himself (Matt. 25:40).

---

9   The addition of $\pi\varepsilon\mu\varphi\theta\acute{\varepsilon}\nu\tau\alpha$ after $\pi\alpha\varrho'\ \acute{\upsilon}\mu\tilde{\omega}\nu$ with F and G, has
been made for the sake of clearness and completeness.

4:19—20

> 19 And my God shall supply every need of yours according to his riches in glory in Christ Jesus.
>
> 20 Now unto our God and Father be the glory for ever and ever. Amen.

19 Not only Paul, but also the Philippians have their needs. And in the same way as they supplied Paul's needs by the gifts they sent him, so God with His gifts and blessings will supply all their needs. This great assurance is given to the Church by the apostle. "My God"—words vibrating with the ring of a personal testimony and confession of faith—"will supply every need of yours," will make provision in His fatherly love and care for all needs material and spiritual, for time and eternity, according to the richness and fulness of His divine providence. He will supply every need "in glory",[1] in a glorious manner whereby His adorable grace and providential love will be revealed "in Christ Jesus." For all benefits and blessings are only experienced in union with Christ and in His fellowship, and are granted in Him and for His sake. In Him there is full provision for all the needs of God's people.

20 In view of the glorious truth of God's fatherly care and provision for His children, a doxology follows. To "our God," the God of Paul and all believers, the God who is

---

[1] The words $\dot{\epsilon}\nu$ $\delta\delta\xi\eta$ must be taken together with $\pi\lambda\eta\varrho\dot{\omega}\sigma\epsilon\iota$. "God will supply in glory, in a glorious manner." The ultimate fulfilment can, of course, also be understood eschatologically as the glorification of the Church which will take place together with Christ's illustrious advent.

"our Father" through Jesus Christ, and who loves and cares for those who are born again of the Spirit to be His children, "be the glory," the inner perfection and its sublime revelation which calls for praise and adoration, "for ever and ever" (literally: for the ages of the ages), for all ages following each other in endless succession, in all eternity.[2]

"Amen" as a closing word serves to approve of what has been said, and is an expression of confirmation and assurance. So it is! Sure and unquestionable! So let it be![3]

---

[2] Such a doxology is often found with Paul (cf. amongst others Rom. 11:36, Gal. 1:5, 1 Tim. 1:17, 2 Tim 4:18).

[3] For the use of *Amen* in the Christian liturgy, in prayers and doxologies, cf. Kittel, I, TWNT, 340 f.

4:21—23

21 Salute every saint in Christ Jesus. The brethren that are with me salute you.

22 All the saints salute you, especially they that are of Caesar's household.

23 The grace of the Lord Jesus Christ be with your spirit.

21 As is usual in his other Letters Paul concludes this Letter with greetings and a benediction. The apostle expresses his loving concern for each individual believer of the Church. "Every saint in Christ Jesus"[1]—for only in Christ and by virtue of His deserts a saved person can be called a saint—must receive the greeting as a sign of fellowship, goodwill and brotherly love. The "brethren" also, who were in contact with Paul during his imprisonment, greet the believers in Philippi. By "brethren" (in contrast with the saints of verse 22) not fellow believers in general are meant here, but in the first instance the fellow workers of Paul in the cause of the gospel, such as Timothy who is mentioned as sender of the Letter together with Paul (1:1; cf. 2:19), and Epaphroditus who is to be the carrier of the Letter to Philippi (2:25—29), and other fellow workers of whom mention is made in 1:14, and who were preachers of the gospel in Rome.

22 The wider circle of believers in Rome is now being

---

[1] ἐν Χρ. ᾽Ιησοῦ should go with πάντα ἅγιον, as in 1:1. If taken together with ἀσπάσασθε, the N. T. expression usually is ἐν κυρίῳ (Rom. 16:22; 1 Cor. 16:19).

referred to and described as "all the saints,"[2] among whom the Christians "of Caesar's household"[3] receive special mention. By this he designates the functionaries and servants and slaves of the Emperor's household, with whom Paul, as a prisoner for several years, undoubtedly came in contact on several occasions, and among whom there were many who accepted the Christian faith as a result of their intercourse with the apostle (cf. 1:12, 13). They—as the spiritual children of the apostle in captivity, and now fellow believers and fellow brethren of the Christians in Philippi—also send their Christian greetings to the Philippians, and at the same time furnish evidence of the progress of the gospel, even in spite of the bonds of the apostle.

23 "The grace of the Lord Jesus Christ (be) with your spirit!"[4] With this benediction or pronouncement of grace the apostle concludes his Letter. "Grace" means unmerited favour, and this is not only the first redeeming gift bestowed by Christ, but it also includes all spiritual blessings which are communicated to man for Christ's sake. The apostle prays that the grace of Christ be with their "spirit", by which man's whole life is governed and which is so very much dependent on God for guidance, safe-keeping, strength and sanctification. "In their whole inner being, in all their thoughts and desires, they must continually share

---

[2] For the objective meaning of "saintly" or "holy," see exposition of 1:1.

[3] By this is not meant the family of the Emperor, or people of high rank and standing at the court. Cf. Lightfoot's note in connection with this, *The Epistle of St. Paul to the Phil.*, pp. 167 and 171 ff.

[4] The reading of K and L (and TR) is μετὰ πάντων ὑμῶν, while that of Aleph A B D E F G P is μετὰ τοῦ πνεύματος ὑμῶν. The A.V. here supports the more unlikely reading.

and experience the grace of the Lord" (Greijdanus). No
benediction more glorious than this with which to conclude
a Letter to a Church of Christ! Amen:[5] So let it be!

---

[5] Aleph A D E and others add ἀμήν to the end of the sentence,
which, however, is wanting with B F G.

As subscription to this Letter Aleph A B have πρὸς Φιλιππησίους,
while with the later K and L it appears in more comprehensive form as
πρὸς Φιλιππησίους ἐγράφη ἀπὸ ʿΡώμης δι᾽ ʾΕπαφροδίτου.

INDEX OF CHIEF SUBJECTS

INDEX OF SCRIPTURE REFERENCES

OLD TESTAMENT

NEW TESTAMENT

INDEX OF SCRIPTURE REFERENCES